A GARLAND

✳✳✳✳✳✳✳✳✳✳✳✳✳✳✳✳✳✳

OF VERSE

To the memory of my precious wife Annice and to our two beloved offspring, Alison and Richard.

A GARLAND
OF VERSE

by

David Payne

Dianthus Publishing Limited

Published by Dianthus Publishing Limited,
The Pool House,
Kemble
Cirencester. GL7 6AD
Tel. 01285 770 239   Fax: 01285 770 896

ISBN 0-946604-25-8

ISBN 978-0-946604-25-8

Preface

by the Rt. Rev. Bishop Morris Maddocks

In his formative book *Learning to Dance* Michael Mayne writes: *Poets help to authenticate what we know most deeply by appealing to our most creative faculty: imagination.* Later he continues *It is our imagination that enables us to see things whole (and holy).*

This collection of poems, written over the course of his life, is testimony to David Payne's profound faith and teasing humour.

His life may have had its ups and downs, but throughout the poems in the first section of this book he perceives the light in the darkness and his faith and hope and love shine through.

His imagination does indeed enable him to see things whole (and holy).

He accentuates his sense of humour and enables us, using our imagination, to laugh along with him and the excellent characters he portrays. For instance, the scene with Canon Bal (dock) -

intoning evensong (at 5)
With ancient canons (still alive)

- will fire our imaginations.

I have known David for nearly thirty years and our friendship has kept alive from those early days when he came as Warden of Crowhurst. We both married an Anne, both of them our better halves.

I am grateful to him for his invitation to write this foreword to his lovely collection of poems and heartily commend it.

Author's Introduction

For many years I have written poetry. The earliest poem, written when I was just nine, is included in this collection. The poems fall loosely into two categories:

Devotional/Serious

Some written at a time of intense angst and suffering.

Humorous

These poems will be of special interest to those who have shared the experiences they describe, for instance those lampooning my fellow members of the Lee Abbey Community (1958/60). I have sought to widen their appeal by a few lines of explanation. In some I have changed surnames to avoid causing offence. It is often said that neurotics and depressives find relief and release in humour. To this I can only plead guilty!

Acknowledgements

I want to pay my respects to my kind friend, Penny Wreford, who has deciphered my appalling handwriting with commendable ability and imagination! A degree in Urdu, Sanskrit or Hebrew would have been of real benefit. She has also typed the poems with great skill and devotion. I am deeply grateful to her.

The Preface has kindly been written by my very dear friend of over 25 years, Bishop Morris Maddocks who, together with his wife Anne, has been an inspiration to me, as to so many, over the years. How much I owe, under God, to him and his wife! Likewise, I am deeply indebted to my Editor, Christian Brann, a youthful octogenarian who has so kindly advised, encouraged and (when necessary) corrected me. I am indeed fortunate to have such a wise and accomplished Editor and such a deeply committed Christian at my side. I thank God from my heart for his wisdom, his professional skill and his prayerful guidance throughout. I could not have found a better nor more sincere friend. Laus Deo!

David Payne

1931   Born in St John's Wood, London NW8.

1936 – 1939   Schooling at Arnold House School, London

1939 – 1945   At The Downs School, Colwall, Nr Malvern, a
                Quaker Prep School where my interest in
                natural history was kindled.

1945 – 1949   At Sherborne School, Sherborne, Dorset.

1950 – 1951   National service in Egypt where I had a
                conversion experience which changed my life.

1951 – 1954   I read natural sciences at Clare College, Cambridge.

1954 – 1957   I taught biology at Marlborough College and Mill Hill
                School, London NW7.

1958 – 1960   Following a time of terrible depression I went to Lee
                Abbey to recover and was wonderfully helped through
                the love and prayers of the community.

1960 – 1962   Attended Wycliffe Hall Theological College, Oxford.

1962   Ordained Deacon in Christ Church, Oxford, by
                Bishop Henry Carpenter.

1963   Ordained Priest in Guildford Cathedral by the Rt Rev
                George Reindorp. Curate of Christ Church, Guildford.

1966 – 1973   Rector of Shackleford and Peper Harrow, Godalming.

1973 – 1978   Rector of Odell and Pavenham near Bedford.

1978 – 1984   Warden of the Crowhurst Home of Christian Healing near Battle, East Sussex.

1984 – 1992   Rector of All Saints, Wraxall, and St Bartholomew's, Failand, near Bristol.

1993 - 1995   Honorary Assistant Curate at St Mary's, Finchley, North London.

1995 -   At South Cerney near Cirencester. Trustee of the Harnhill Centre for Christian Healing.

DEVOTIONAL AND SERIOUS POEMS

Journey To The Water's Edge

The Muntjak Deer

Odell, Bedfordshire, 1976

This poem, written in free verse (unusually, for me) was inspired by the rare sight of one or two of these very shy little deer coming down Church Lane, past our Rectory, to drink from the River Ouse. This was occasioned by the drying up of their water holes in The Great Wood, some 3/4 mile above us.

Long hidden in the Great Wood once there lived
The Chinese barking deer, (as some would say).
Not natives of this land, they yet have found   .
This refuge in the wood.
Escaped from Woburn Park or some great country house
Maybe in war time years.
Hidden most oft to view, retiring, shy,
Fearful of human voice or form,
Deep denizens of thicket and woodland,
Forest creatures in the main,
Rarely they issued forth.
Yet this shy herd, seen only by the keeper and his dogs,
Preferring hidden growth and leafy shade
Were seldom seen by man, save crossing once the glade,
Finding their food and water in the wood.
By custom this wood had become their sylvan home.
Labelled on ancient maps "Wood Hill",
(Hence Woodhill, Odell now for many years),
And guarded safe this little herd, giving them
Needed sanctuary of hidden peace.

Rarely they ventured forth, finding sufficiency
Of food and water in the wood.
Yet then, in summer of '76, the long hot summer of drought

With field and pasture burnt by searing sun,
Their woodland waterhole (we think) had failed.
And they, the shy retiring creatures of the wood,
(The Great Wood be it noted on the map)
Urged on by desperate thirst, would tiptoe forth at dawn
And wind their timid way with hurried step down Old Church Lane,
Seeking fresh waters from the River Ouse.

Not once or twice but several times we spied them
Hurrying down the lane,
These tiny hunting creatures of the night.
They, at half light or when the mists at dawn
Lay heavy o'er the fields,
Risking exposure now they tiptoed, nervous, yet brave in quest,
Past Yelnow (Keepers Cottage), Hobbs Green,
And those old thatched cottages (no more than half a dozen)
Leading toward the river.
Shy little creatures! Yet such their thirst
That they this fearsome pilgrimage must make at break of dawn
To drink clear water from the river's edge,
And there (we guess) unseen they'd slake their raging thirst
With long cool drafts of water as they stood,
And hinds with burning tongue would
Drink with deep delight.
We picture them astride the river bank,
Shy, nervous, twitching at the brink,
Slaking their thirst so keenly at the water's edge,
Not once but many times they drank
From that wide river, fresh and cool at dawn.
And then they'd pause and stare, refreshed,
The water dripping from their muzzles
And nostrils wet and shining, by the willows' shade.
Contented now they'd quietly turn,
Skipping across the village road,
And shyly tiptoe past our Rectory home,
Up old Church Lane,
Before the sun had risen o'er sleeping Felmersham.

Few saw their journey home,
And few we think have guessed
The awful peril of that pilgrimage
And what it cost them, courage born of thirst.
Shy little creatures from another land,
They'd made this pilgrimage of grace
To find refreshment, having left the place
Where once they dwelled.
Yes, these small creatures of the woodland home
Had risked their all to find
That which both doe and hind most surely need:
Pure streams of grace.

Shall we who've witnessed this pilgrimage
Not learn a lesson from this scene?
Dear Saviour Christ has taught us in his word
That all who come to him a-thirst
Shall drink from Him rivers of living water
There shall flow from deep within.
And all who dare to make this pilgrimage
Down to the water's edge, their thirst assuage
With his life-giving stream.

The Pilgrim's Chapel

This was created in the year of centenary (1987) at St Bartholomew's, Failand, near Bristol. A copy still hangs (I believe) next to the tapestry.

Pause, gentle pilgrim, as you come today
And kneel a moment, silent, here to pray.
This tapestry of Chaucer's men on pilgrimage
Is not just history of a distant age,
It is His story for all men to read.
How we who journey on through life still need
To listen to the voice of one who said,
"I am the way that all mankind should tread.
I am the life, the life once given for thee.
I am the truth, the truth that sets men free.

I am the fellow pilgrim who once trod
The self-same journey as the Son of God.
I walked the dusty roads of Palestine,
My feet were weary, wounded just as thine,
Torn by sharp flints then nailed upon the tree.
Oh, fellow pilgrim, pause now, look and see
In those dear wounded feet and nail-pierced hands
The saving token of my love's sweet bands.
Pause to consider 'midst this passing age
How I, your Saviour, meet you on your pilgrimage
As fellow traveller journeying on the road
That leads you to your Saviour and your God.
Pause and remember how, in Holy Week,

I took a towel and washed disciples' feet.
Kneel to remember how in an upper room
I stooped and knelt to touch the feet of loved ones whom
I'd chosen as companions on the way
That led them through the cross to Easter Day."

So let this Chapel be the pilgrim's rest
Where weary ones may pause and be refreshed.
And may the risen Jesus Christ this day
Bless, guard, protect and keep you on the way.

The 8 am Eucharist At St Julian's

Coolham, Sussex.

In the night I had been through great darkness and angst, but when I drew the curtains the sun shone brilliantly and I felt a huge relief as I prepared to partake in the Eucharist.

For long I'd lain, the night time seemed unending,
Veil of dark mist upon my soul forlorn.
Storm on my soul, and anguished heart cries rending.
Silent my soul, before the coming dawn.

So long my soul in night's cold mist lay darkened,
Night of dark fear before the breaking dawn.
I drew the curtains, saw the sun majestic
Shine forth upon those hills; another day is born!

Curtain of mist now gladly drawn asunder,
Christ from His cross proclaims the veil is torn.
And as on distant hills the sunshine's splendour,
So in my heart the risen Christ is born.

He bids me come to kneel before His table,
There to proclaim with sacred bread and wine,
That He the Lord born once within the stable
Now shares with us His mystic life divine.

We kneeling wait, in silent love adoring,
He now the Host unseen amidst us stands.
He comes in love, His sacred heart outpouring,
Ready to fill our outstretched empty hands.

So, Lord, we kneel before thine altar,
Hungry our souls before this throne of thine.
O feed us, Lord, whose lives so often falter
With these sweet gifts of sacred love divine.

Food for our souls we weary pilgrims cry for,
Drink for our thirst, the mystic cup of wine.
We here the ones whom Jesus came to die for,
We chosen guests, and He the Host divine.

So now we come, our feeble hands outreaching,
Silent our souls before the throne of God.
O grant us, Lord, to feed upon thy body
And drink of thee in sacred wine, thy blood.

Bread of thy body grant us for thy healing
And brimming cup, thy chalice filled with wine.
We kneel before thine altar, wondrous feeling,
Ourselves the branches, he the ancient vine.

See now the sun upon the sanctuary shining
On all who come with needy souls athirst.
Here now the Saviour God with man is dining,
He now the 'second Adam' feeds the first.

We raise our eyes, and now with hearts entrusted,
Empty the Cross engraved in clearest glass.
We see the oak with lichened boughs encrusted,
His sacred footprints touch the shining grass.

See how He stands upon the lake-shore,
A song thrush now so gladly sings,
Reminding us that our most glorious Saviour
Is risen now with healing in His wings.

Soaring

*We would watch these lovely birds of prey soaring effortlessly above us,
over the woods above Wraxall Rectory where I was Rector from 1984-1992.*

I see the buzzard soar and wonder why
He finds such easeful passage through the sky.
Why, when we earthbound creatures heave and plod,
Should he ascend so lightly up to God?

Easeful he soars above on outstretched wings,
Circling upon the thermals, rising brings
All heaven and earth within his orbit round.
Why, Lord, should he ascend yet I be bound?

"Child, I have given you wings of faith and prayer.
Why don't you spread those wings, why don't you dare
To reach those pinions wide? Then you shall ride
The heavens and, like the angel host,
Circle the heavenly place; then you shall coast

Like buzzards on the soaring air.
The upflow of my Spirit then shall bear
You to my dwelling place, and on the tide
Of my great love you too shall ride.
Borne as on eagle's wings, you too shall see my face
And soar with me in realms of endless grace."

So when you see the buzzard in the sky
Soaring majestic, easeful, up on high,
Know that you too who earthbound plod
Are called to spread your wings and mount to God.

Prayer For Troubled Mariners

At Lyme Regis, one of our favourite holiday places long ago, the contrast of dark clouds and a glorious flaming sunset spoke volumes to my wife, Anne, and myself.

Lord of all being, throned on high,
Thy glory flames o'er sea and sky.
The sunset burning in the west
Proclaims to distant lands, "How blessed."

Thy voice is heard upon the waves,
The glory of the name that saves.
Deep unto deep tells of thy power
At stormy sunset's fiery hour.

As storm clouds low'r upon the deep,
O Saviour, in thy mercy keep
All those who travel there by night,
Shed on their journey heavenly light.

Guard, dearest Saviour, in thine arms
Those who in tempest wild alarms
'Midst rock and shoal and angry sea
Toil on their journey home to thee.

When night's dark shadows o'er them lie,
And storm and tempest round them cry,
Shed forth thy light upon them till
They hear thy voice saying, "Peace, be still."

Lord, who hast made these troubled seas,
Their journey guide, their passage ease.
When midnight comes and darkest hour,
Keep them, dear Saviour, by thy power.

Teach them, O Lord, who ruled the waves
The wonder of the Name that saves.
Reveal, O Lord, amidst the storm
The wonder of the Saviour's form.

Shed on their path in blackest night
The radiance of a Saviour's light.
And show them in their hour of trial
The beauty of the Saviour's smile.

O thou who once didst tread the storm
As God's anointed Son upborne
By arms unseen above the wave,
Teach us the name that still can save!

Teach us the truth that Jesus reigns
Amidst our earthly toils and pains.
Guide our frail bark till breaks the dawn
With splendour of an Easter morn.

Glory Now Be To God

This was written as my wife, Anne, and I watched the sun setting over the Welsh hills. Time and again, after difficult times in the parish of Wraxall, we would drive down to Clevedon and gaze across the Bristol Channel, watching the sunset. The reflection of the rays of the setting sun reminded us keenly of the God who 'walks on the waves'.

Glory now be to God for sunset flaming,
The wide expansive sweep of sky and sea.
Glory now be to God for hills and mountains
Whose rugged grandeur spells His majesty.

Glory now be to God for troubled waters,
The channel angry, storm clouds scudding west.
Glory now be to Him who brought us
Through tribulation to His perfect rest.

Glory now be to God for ocean's splendour
And gleam of sunshine gold on distant hills.
Glory now be to God for all His grandeur,
The Lord who tames the tempest, wild waves stills.

Glory now be to God for all creation,
The sweep of seagulls o'er the breaking waves.
Glory now be to God! Each generation
Proclaims afresh the mighty God who saves.

Glory now be to God for flight of curlew,
Sea-pies, all anxious, crying on the shore.
Glory now be to God for evening's curfew,
Dusk-fall of silence midst the ocean's roar.

Glory now be to God for evening vessels
Slipping their silent passage through the sea.
Glory to God who gives them needed refuge,
Haven and harbour safe for all who flee.

So now at dusk we see the ocean's grandeur.
Storm clouds hang dark, yet sun-gleam breaking through
Lights up a pathway. 'Tis the Lord in splendour!
He walks upon the waves, majestic too.

"Peace now", he says, "amidst your tribulation.
Peace now e'er earthly storms shall cease.
This is my word of wondrous new creation,
I come to you, the mighty Prince of Peace.

The Eucharist: Easter Day at Patching

In Memory of Henry Coles

This was written in memory of a very dear friend, Henry Coles, for his wife and family. An uncle of my wife, now 95, recalls seeing the last surviving working oxen at Exceat Farm, Seaford, in 1921. He was riding on the top of an open bus.

While Easter bread is broken, wine outpoured,
We come to make communion with our blessed Lord.
Here in this ancient church, His dwelling place,
We seek in hour of need His wondrous grace.
Silent He comes, and with this precious food
Would feed us with His body and his blood.

Here priest and people through the passing years
Have sought their God in turmoil and in tears.
Drover and carter, shepherd, ploughman, child,
Sweet solace here have found in tempest wild.
And where the oxen ploughed in plodding team,
And where the plover dived with frenzied scream,
They to this holy place have come apart
To meet the risen Lord with humble heart.

Some to this quiet place have come to weep
While others silent vigil at the altar keep.
Ploughboy and shepherd, herdsman, coachman, squire,
Here too have knelt beside the ancient choir.
Each to this table blest have quietly trod
The rugged pathway to the throne of God.

So now you kneel, but empty is his place,
Where once you both did kneel, a space.
You long to touch your loved one, hold his hand,
And in this sacred place once more to stand

Together for a while; yet now the loss
So bitter-sweet shall draw you to the cross.
The Saviour Lord, the man of sorrows too,
His nail-pierced hands reach out in love to you.
His cry of dereliction you can hear,
It tells you that your risen Lord is near.

Once then, like Mary, shrouded in the gloom
On Easter morn you gaze within Christ's tomb,
And there, within the space his garments rolled
And linen napkin, stands an angel bold.
"Woman", he says, "Why weep you now for He
The Easter Lord is risen, oh turn and see!"

And she, supposing him to be the gardener there
Looks on him smiling, gentle, fair.
"Tell me, good sir", she says, "If you did take
My Lord away, for him my heart doth break."
"Mary!", he says, and she in wonder lost
Answers "Rabboni". He whom she loved most

Stands in the garden, radiant, smiling face,
And bids her step into that sunlit place.
"Oh, touch me not", he says, "For I've not yet
Ascended to my Father. Hasten now and let
My brethren know that I who once did lay
Within this tomb, this glorious Easter Day
Am risen now! Victorious o'er the strife
I stand with you, the wondrous Lord of Life!

That empty tomb, your ache of human loss
I can redeem, for now beneath my cross
The husk shall die, but out of this the corn
Of new life glorious springs on Easter morn!
So come again and kneel in sacred tryst,
I come to you in joyful Eucharist.
Solace and comfort, grace and strength provide,
I, Jesus, live, who once was crucified!

And you shall know before my altar dear
The presence of your loved ones, oh, so near.
The veil that seems to lie 'twixt earth and heaven
Is parted now, for by my cross 'tis riven.
Gold glory breaks and angels gathered round,
The music of a thousand voices sound
The praises of our God in majesty,
Complete in him the glorious tapestry!

And Jesus Looked On Peter

**To my good friend, Peter Vaughan,
on his consecration as Bishop of Ramsbury in Salisbury Cathedral**

We came, the members of that mighty throng
Who gathered there to kneel along
With you. And in that quiet holy place
To pray with you that, strengthened by his grace,
You whom the Lord has called might be
Endowed with gifts of true *episcope*.
We knelt with you on this most wondrous day
And pledged ourselves alongside you to pray
That as he called you Peter, Man of Rock,
He now will bless you, guardian of his flock.

And as you knelt before the throne of grace
To make your vows 'fore him, the Lord's dear face
Smiled on you kindly as you trembling knelt
Within this great cathedral, and we felt
His hand of blessing on you quietly laid
As you those solemn vows so clearly made.
And as the choir did lovely anthems sing
You pledged yourself to Him, the servant King.

Pause then a moment in the upper room,
Last refuge 'fore his cross and earthly tomb,
He lays aside his garments, takes a towel
And pours out water 'to the humble bowl.
Then with those loving hands, the dusty feet
Of twelve disciples washes there. How sweet
This ministry of his with love outpoured
Who calls you now to follow him, the servant Lord.
Stripped of all glory, he the servant kneels
To bathe those weary feet. O how he feels
The pain of pilgrim feet who've bravely trod
The rugged pathway to the throne of God.

And you a Bishop in his Church are called to be
A servant of the Lord, in great humility.
To teach, admonish, feed and guard the flock
And build them up on him, the Ancient Rock.
Who is sufficient for this awesome task?
That's why we, kneeling there, did humbly ask
That of his mercy he will now supply
The gifts and grace of true *episcope*.

And when the battle's fierce, the tumult strong,
We trust you will recall that mighty throng
Who knelt with you on this most wondrous day
And pledged ourselves along with you to pray.
So may the hand of God upon you ever rest
And may you, as a servant dear, be ever blessed.

Apple of my Eye

(A meditation on Deuteronomy 32, 9-14)

When in the wilderness my people faced
The agony of desert place and howling waste,
There I encircled you with love divine
And gently sought you, dearest child of mine.
I know the desert places you have known,
I came to seek you, loved one, as my own.
There I encircled you in the wilderness
And sought to touch you with my love's caress.
There in that desert place so harsh and dry
I kept you even as the 'apple of my eye'.
There, like an eagle fluttering near its young,
I flew beneath you while you fearful clung,
Spreading my pinions 'neath you, angel's wings,
I bore you up majestic, King of Kings.
I made you ride on high in realms of grace
Until at last you saw my Father's face.
I fed you sweetest honey from the rock,
Curds from the herd and milk from my dear flock.
Yes, I the Shepherd God, the great I AM,
Have journeyed with you through your desert, precious lamb.
There on dark Calvary I shed my blood
And gave my life for you, the lamb of God.
For bread of life I gave you the finest wheat
And for your thirst the gift of wine so sweet.
Red blood of grape you drank, crushed on the precious vine,
O taste and see, this is my love divine.
I in the wilderness and the desert place
Have come to you my wounded child with grace.
Grace now sufficient, I your Lord am nigh.
I smile on you in love, the 'apple of my eye.'

Borne As On Eagle's Wings

Deuteronomy 32, v.11

Borne as on eagle's wings, thou Lord my stay,
Teach me to rest in thee each passing day.
Borne as on eagle's wings, whate'er betide
Lord help me, close to thee let me abide.
Borne as on eagle's wings, Lord give me grace
Quietly to rest in thy safe dwelling place.
Borne as on eagle's wings, through storm and strife
Teach me to hide in thee, Lord of my life.
Borne as on eagle's wings, teach me to soar,
O lift me heavenwards, thee to adore.
Borne as on eagle's wings, swift through the air
Teach me to ride with thee, safe in thy care.
Borne as on eagle's wings, when storm clouds darken
Teach me to hear thy voice, my soul to harken.
Borne as on eagle's wings, when storm clouds break
Teach me to shelter there, for thy name's sake.
Borne as on eagle's wings, 'midst Satan's lies
Lift thou me heavenwards, up to the skies.
Borne as on eagle's wings, far above strife,
Keep me in victory, Lord of my life.
Borne as on eagle's wings, when I'm afraid
Help me to trust, Lord; on thee I am stayed.

Borne as on eagle's wings, my spirit sings
High in the heavenly place. Thou King of Kings,
Bear thou me heavenwards through realms of grace.
Then in thy mercy, Lord, show me thy face.
When all earth's storms are o'er, vanquished all strife,
Then let me dwell with thee, Lord of my life.

George and Pamela

Dedicated to dear friends of mine for over 40 years on the occasion of their silver wedding, 1 April 1989.

Since at St Giles you two young things were wed,
I can't remember much as mere Best Man,
My duties on that day (I think) quite smoothly ran.
George, I remember, dining out to lunch
Choked on the chips and peas which we did munch.
"I can't eat any more", he said, pale round the gorge.
"Oh never mind", I said, "You'll manage, George!"

Then to the Church (I think it was St Giles)
We ventured forth, all top hats, frock coats, smiles.
We took our place, George trembling at the brink
Of holy matrimony. What did Pamela think?
The organ changed its tune, the Bridal March
Resounded loud, and George's lips did parch.
The doors swung open, Pamela clad in white,
Bride of his dreams, hove gently into sight.
George from his pew (we think he nearly died)
Stepped trembling out, the Best Man at his side.
And there was Pamela, smiling, radiant, pink,
And, spying George, gave him a knowing wink!

The service starts, the bridesmaids waiting stand.
One takes the bridal bouquet in her hand.
"Dearly beloved, we are gathered here
To join this man and woman. Now, pray do not fear,
Young George, this woman here to take
To be thy wedded wife. She'll surely make
A helpmeet and a loving partner who
From bachelor ways will surely rescue you!"

"George, wilt thou take this woman fair to be
Thy wedded wife in lifelong matrimony?"
George, swallowing back a frozen pea (quite chill)
Speaks out quite boldly, "Yes, I surely will!"

"And Pamela, now will you this handsome cleric take
To be your wedded husband, and then make
Your wedding vows on this your nuptial day,
Him most devotedly to cherish, love, obey?"
The bride then turning to the groom, serene and smiling still,
Addresses him in dulcet tones, "Of course, you know I will!"
Rings are exchanged, the promises are made.
(I'm not quite sure if Pamela has obeyed!)
Then, as they pause, the bridegroom and the bride,
Their hands are joined, the sacred knot is tied.

The registers are signed! The deed is done!
The Wedding March is played, and forth they come.
George smiling shyly as they tread the aisle,
While Pamela displays a radiant smile.
The church bells peal! The doors are open wide!
Proudly they stand, the bridegroom and the bride.
Wild bells, ring out! All Oxford's gathered here,
And thousands in the 'Gilers' start to cheer!
George, once the lovely Pamela's suitor,
Is Wycliffe Hall's most newly married tutor!

The passing years have fled, and now by grace
We've gathered here in this most lovely place
To render thanks 'midst all the passing years
For times of joyous laughter, suffering, tears,
Two lovely children, parishes much blessed,
The years of ministry and times of rest,
Rainbow and sunshine, threatening storm and cloud.
We, chosen guests, part of the greater crowd
Who shared your nuptials many years ago,
We join with you, and want you both to know
That you're much loved, and in our hearts we pray
God's richest blessing on your wedding day.

Golden Wedding

Desmond and Vida Hignett.

Desmond was my much-loved church warden at St Mary's Church,
Shackleford near Godalming, and a very keen cricketer.

Dear friends, on this your wedding day
We're gathered here with you to say
That five decades of 'holy mat'
Is something not to be sniffed at!
'Tis fifty years, we've heard it said,
Since you young things were truly wed.

You, Desmond, then a city lad,
Neat, trim and dapper and well clad
In morning dress and grey top hat
Were quite a figure to gaze at.
And Vida, you the blushing bride
Our Desmond's joy and lifelong pride.
The year (I think) was '39.
West Indies under Constantine
Delighted crowds both near and far
Amidst the threat of Hitler's war.
When storm clouds gathered o'er the west
You two decided it was best
To join your hands, whate'er might be,
In glad and glorious matrimony.

And so began (forgive the quip)
Your finest 'opening partnership'.
Today it's time for us to swear
You have achieved, well, something rare:

One hundred runs (that's fifty each),
A lesson you could England teach!
Like Hobbs and Sutcliffe in time past

You've weathered many a stormy blast.
Your partnership delights us all
Who gather here in Village Hall,
And with your much loved family
We hope the best is yet to be.
Oh yes, we know you've had to graft
For every run, and yet a shaft
Of golden light breaks forth today
Falling on you, at 'close of play'.

We know you joined the 'boys in blue'
And served with many a gallant crew,
While you a handsome Squadron Leader
Had at your side the precious Vida.
When Hitler'd done with knavish tricks
You were demobbed in '46.
Once more in city suit now clad
You off to Lord's would sometimes gad.
And while the mounting score did climb
You kept an eye on Father Time.

Now this golden age's begun
We know you're counting every run.
Fifty not out is quite a score,
We trust that there'll be many more
Fine flowing strokes from you two dears.
This opening stand, full fifty years,
Has been a partnership so blessed
And one that's clearly stood the test.
Like Donald Bradman past his ton,
We sense the game has just begun.
And though the going has been hard
It's time you both took a fresh guard.
No more the time like Gower and Pringle
To scamper youthfully for a single.
The spirit's strong, the limbs grow weary,
No more you'll pounce like the great Leary!

And now the stands behind the Mound
Have cast long shadows o'er the ground.
The scoreboard reads, without a doubt,
'Desmond and Vida – 50 not out'!
'Ere Father Time removes the bails,
Though eyesight dims and memory fails,
You will recall, though p'raps not fully,
The golden age of Frank T Woolley,
Whom as a youth young Desmond saw
Caught at long on for 94!

So here before the seasons pass
We bid you stand and raise a glass.
"The bride and bridegroom" is the toast!
Desmond and Vida whom we love most.
For you two souls we humbly pray
God bless you on your 'golden day'!

Good Friday – It is Done!

This is a meditation before the cross of Jesus, written prior to the author leading a Devotion of Three Hours.

Peace now descends, the Saviour's life surrendered
To his dear Father on that awesome cross.
Peace now for Him who glad obedience rendered
Perfect forgiving love in hour of loss.

Peace now descends on Him who gladly suffered
The perfect sacrifice of life so freely given,
His heart of love in full obedience offered,
The stricken rock for all mankind is riven.

Noble in death, in this most loving duty
He bows his head, the full surrender made.
And there they see their King, now crowned in beauty,
Bound to that cross, the Father's will obeyed.

"Father", he says, "I now commend my spirit
Into thy loving hands most glad and free.
Accept my love in this life's final offering,
I here surrender all my life to thee."

The soldiers come, to him no comfort bringing,
And with a sword-thrust pierce his broken heart.
There flows forth blood and water, sweet commingling
Is here revealed. The waiting crowds depart.

They see His cross, but see no more His visage,
His bleeding head is bowed, his body torn.
They came to mock a man, they see a Saviour,
His kingly head now crowned with glorious thorn.

And did they know, the ones who shared his story,
The ones who now this deed of shame have done,
Did they perceive in him the Prince of Glory,
God's chosen one, beloved and only Son?

So Mary kneels, in anguished love adoring,
Broken by grief, the silent tears flow down
Watering the earth, her mother's love outpouring,
A sword thrust through her heart, sweet suffering's crown.

The crowds disperse, the soldiers come to take Him,
Draw out the nails, remove the piercing thorn,
And from that rugged cross which so did break Him,
They lay Him on the ground, God's only Son.

And then they bear Him, lifeless, to the garden.
He who was born of Mary's loving womb,
Is now laid down, securing all men's pardon,
And buried there in Joseph's rock-hewn tomb.

There at the tomb, as love's most tender duty,
Last rites of burial so lovingly perform.
They lay Him there, this life of perfect beauty,
The wondrous Son of God in human form.

The tomb is closed, with rock its entrance sealed,
And there the soldiers mount a watching guard,
Until the glory of the Lord shall be revealed
On Easter Day, His royal way is barred.

Good Friday 1993

Veiled by dark fear, my wounded spirit cries.
Unto the wounded Christ I lift my eyes.
Pierced on the cross amidst the darkness He,
None now can fathom full such agony.

He, hanging there all helpless on the cross,
Alone can penetrate my deepest loss.
Pierced with the thorns, He from the cross descends
To darkest hell, and there my spirit mends.

The serpent's head is crushed, his fangs are drawn,
The poison stenched, so Satan suffers scorn.
There Jesus bleeds, all wounded on the tree
That brings me life, such awful mystery.

The antidote for sin, his precious blood,
The gift outpoured by Jesus, Son of God.
There on the cross in beauty stark revealed
The Saviour God who now mankind has healed.

Look on His brow, His hands, His feet, His side,
Those precious wounds our healing shall provide,
Cleansing from sin, the guilt all purged away,
Cancelled the debt, there's now an open way.

Wounded His heart of love, His arms reached wide,
We refuge take within the Saviour's side.
Blessed now by grace, His heart by swordthrust riven,
"It's done!", He cries. Our sins are all forgiven.

I kneeling come, my head bowed low, my pride
I lay beneath the cross where Jesus died.
Gone now my sins, He opens wide His arms
Embraces me with arms of love; my spirit calms.

"O child forlorn", He says, "Why did you rage
Against my love? I long to assuage
Your pain and anguish in my love's embrace.
I'll fold you close, look up and see my face.

My name is LOVE. Oh, see the sacred wounds.
There is no limit to my love, no bounds
Where you may stray unsought. Where'er you flee
I follow after you – both love and mystery.

I, Jesus Christ, who once upon the cross
Poured out my all for you. There is no loss
Or pain I have not felt, your anguished tears
I've wept with you. I'll calm all foolish fears.

David the name, beloved of the Lord,
You too have known the piercing of the sword.
Wounded, you sought to earn my love. Yet I decree
It comes as gift, O wondrous mystery!

Come then, my son, and let me now embrace
The wounded child within. Look at my face,
There is no anger there, just love's sweet smile.
Allow me to enfold you as a child.

My love, like Mary's love, is 'El Shaddai',
The all sufficient one. Ah, sweetest mystery
Of love revealed which Jesus knew as child caressed,
Enfolded there asleep on Mary's breast.

This is my heart's desire: that you should rest
Within the folding of my love caressed.
This is my gift to you. Such love divine
Shall never cease – just know that you are mine."

Journey's End: Dawn Breaks in Lyme Regis

"Whose way is in the seas."

Now burns the glory of the rising sun,
Now praise we that the night is gone.
Gone the dark terror of rock and shoal,
Here now rest we in port, our haven goal.

Full flows the tide and wide the ocean's sweep,
Storm clouds are vanished, now upon the deep
Comes there great peace again, tranquil the waters lie,
Still at the Master's voice, "Peace, it is I."

Far in the east proud cliffs majestic rise,
Bastions of rock unmoved against the cries
Of stormy sea, wave crash in midnight hour,
Telling afresh the mighty Saviour's power.

Now dance the sunbeams on the sparkling tide,
Now floods the sunrise o'er the ocean wide.
Sun, sky and ocean now with one accord
Proclaim the glory of the risen Lord.

Rock, shoal and tempest have done their worst,
Now Jesus reigns in power, His foes dispersed.
Rules He, majestic Lord of sea and sky,
His praise we sing, His name we laud on high.

Now each frail bark secure from wind and storm
Safe lies at port within the harbour's arm.
Calm and serene the weary sailors sleep,
Far from the fury of the tossing deep.

Teach us , O Saviour, who once the waves did tame,
Always to keep within the refuge of thy name,
Always to rest within the haven of thy word,
Always to trust thee, risen conquering Lord.

Teach us, dear Lord, when clouds have hid thy sun
To praise thy name, O thou most holy one.
Teach us each day with one accord to sing
The glories of our risen Lord and King.

Lord of the Passing Years

Lord of the passing years, whom we adore,
We humbly ask for grace to love thee more.
Through storm and tempest many years have flown,
Our love for thee so cold has oft-times grown.

Too oft in days of travail and distress
We've wandered faithless in the wilderness.
Too oft when suffering comes with searing pain
We've turned from thee, thy love we did disdain.

Too oft when trials sore and Satan pressed
We've fled from thee, and other gods confessed.
Too oft in wilfulness we've disobeyed
And from the pathway of thy will have strayed.

Too oft when flesh was weak and spirit failed
Before the hosts of Satan we have quailed.
Too oft when shadows of thy cross did fall
We fearful fled, when Calvary did call.

Too oft when fires of hell and suffering burned
We've turned from thee and thy sweet love have spurned.
Too oft we've failed in times of bitter loss
To taste the sweetness of thy saving cross.

Too oft when loved ones come to comfort us
We've turned away, rejecting thus thy cross.
Too oft when life has called we've looked askance
And, chained by fear, have failed to join the dance.

Too oft when music and sweet laughter's rung
We to our private griefs have fearful clung.
Too oft when offered comfort, love's embrace,
We've turned from thee, hiding a tear-stained face.

Too oft when offered love, we've craven fled
And turned away, while thy sweet love hath bled.
Too oft when called to loneliness and loss
We've failed to share in this thy lonely Cross.

Lord of the passing years, too long we've spent
These years of faithlessness, we now repent
And ask thee, by thy grace, each bitter loss
To turn to glorious gain, by thy sweet cross.

Lord of the passing years, help us to grasp
The offer of thy love, each day to clasp
The outstretched hand of Him who died,
The wounded hand of Him, the crucified.

Lord of the passing years, once lifted high,
Teach us like grains of wheat just how to die,
How to say "No" to self and "Yes" to thee,
How, Lord, to share thy wondrous Calvary.

Teach us, good Lord, who for us sinners died,
To live and reign in Him, the crucified!
Lord of the passing years, whom we adore,
O give us grace to love thee more and more.

Lyme Regis: Sunshine In Winter

This was a favourite holiday place for us.

Lord of Creation and Father Almighty
This day we praise thee for all thou hast given.
Wonder of ocean and blue skies above us,
White clouds a-scudding o'er distant horizons,
Crash of the waves and white flight of seagulls,
Sun-drenched sea-shore and sands clean and glistening.
Chatter of children excited and free,
Wide-eyed with wonder, dabbling in streamlets,
Laughing, excited, spontaneous, delighted,
Dogs all a-barking, chasing in frenzy,
Spume-break on gumboots, anoraks colourful.
Glory of Stone Barrow, Golden Cap, Chesil Beach,
Shadow of Portland, e'en distant Purbeck,
White-rimmed with breakers, all spent on their journeying,
Messengers spume-laden far out to sea.
Glint of wet golden sand, trickle of rivulet,
Breakwaters, rock pools and fresh footprints oceanwards,
Call of the 'sea-pie' and cry of the sea.
Yachts all laid up in quiet preparation,
Waiting for springtime and call of the ocean wave,
Ready to slip down and glide through the sea.
Here is my heart-cry, O Lord of Creation,
You who have called us to fresh liberty.

Blows the wind icily now on the cliff tops,
Hidden, majestic, yet wondrous is He
Who fashions the Earth with his glorious majesty.
Seascape and landscape, earth, sky and sea,
Lord of Creation we listen with wonder
All you have given us is gloriously free.
Move by your spirit and teach us to praise thee
Move by thy spirit and help us to see

Thou art the Lord of this glorious creation,
Lord of the stars, the sky and the sea.
Why should we cower like slaves behind prison bars
When your dear Son by his blood set us free?
Free to proclaim thee, the Lord of Creation,
Mover of ocean wave, how can it be
We should not recognise signs of thy goodness,
Maker and giver of divine artistry?

We who have wasted like vessels in winter
Grey as old hulks so encrusted and worn
Winter blight, barnacled, weary with salt spray,
Touch, Lord, these vessels in winter forlorn,
Touch, Lord, and loose them out of their harbours,
Ready to sail on the crest of the ocean,
Breasting the waves like gulls on the wing again.
Father, dear Father, pray set all such free,
Free us from 'shore-hugging', hiding in harbours,
Move by thy spirit and cause us to be
Bold as a galleon that speeds on the waters.
Cleanse and relaunch us in service of thee,
Take away craven fears, silence our trembling,
Move by thy spirit and help us to be
Free as the seagulls who soar ever heavenwards
Answering the call of the wind and the sea.
Lord of all life you have called us to freedom
Grant us a spirit so willing and free
Ready to sail from the safety of harbours
Of craven fearing and timidity.
Into that freedom of sons of the Father
Who gave us his Son to set our souls free,
Free from the shackles of sin and of sickness
Shedding his life blood for you and for me.

Now we would praise thee for days of such wonder.
Great God, creator of earth, sky and sea,
Come in thy power as we give thee the glory
Sunset a'flaming thy glory proclaiming,
Lord of our lives come and set our souls free
Grant that in seeing thy wondrous creation
All glory and praise shall be given to thee.

Meditation on Psalm 23

Lord be my faithful shepherd now
And lead me in these days
To pastures green and waters still,
Where I may learn thy ways.

Lord lead me to those pastures green
Where I may quietly rest,
And take me to the water's edge
To drink and be refreshed.

Too long I've known the desert way
And struck the rocks in vain.
For living streams of water fresh
My soul cries out again.

Oh, lead me to the fountains fair,
My soul is parched and dry.
My soul's athirst for thee my God,
Dear Saviour, hear my cry!

My thirsty soul doth truly pine
For streams of flowing grace.
Oh, lead me to the fount divine
And let me taste thy grace.

How oft I've strayed from the strait path
Of thy dear will divine.
Oh, lead me back in Jesus' way,
I put my hand in thine.

Oh, lead me to the waters, Lord,
Where I may pause to take
Cool draughts of crystal water clear,
My burning thirst to slake.

Oh, Jesus Lord, I've known such fears
And trials beyond belief.
Why is it, Lord, I come to thee
Yet cannot find relief?

For I have sought to love thee, Lord,
For seven and thirty years.
Why is it, Lord, I've known so much
Of conflict, pain and tears?
The Lord looks down on you, my son.
He says, "My child, so blessed,
Come unto me, you weary one,
And I will give you rest.

Too oft you've looked for human love
From friends the very best.
Oh, come to me, my precious child,
And I will give you rest."

A Meditation At Eventide

When westward sinks the setting sun
And all the earth is blessed,
I hear the voice of Jesus say
"Come unto me and rest."

When storm clouds lower and skies are dark
And I am sore distressed,
I hear the voice of Jesus say
"Come unto me and rest."

When doubts assail and Satan seeks
To put me to the test,
I hear the voice of Jesus say
"Come unto me and rest."

When faith grows dim and flesh is weak
And I am sorely pressed,
I hear the voice of Jesus say
"Come unto me and rest."

When I have failed to love Him much,
Poor fledgling in his nest,
I hear the voice of Jesus say
"Come unto me and rest."

When at his table I would dine
I come at His behest,
And hear the voice of Jesus say
"Come unto me and rest."

When earthly comforts fade away
In love I am caressed,
I hear the voice of Jesus say
"Come unto me and rest."

When I now tired and weary lay
My head upon his breast,
I hear the voice of Jesus say
"Come unto me and rest."

When I am still and hear His voice
Then I am truly blessed,
He says those loving words to me
"Come unto me and rest."

When life is done, my journey run,
I have but one request:
That I may hear His own dear Son
Say, "Enter now my rest."

Ode to St Bart'lemew at Failand

(With apologies to Sir John Betjeman)

A sculpture was commissioned for the Church's centenary in 1987. The first draft sketch made him look very severe.

Saint Bart'lemew amidst the pine
We all agree is rather fine.
Bald pate a-shining after rain
And noble brow (like Mr Payne?)
He in his cosy niche the while
Displays a beatific smile.

But th'apostle first we knew
The figure that our artist drew
With butcher's knife and jaw quite tough,
We all agreed was frightfully rough.
The kind of villain you might meet
At dead of night in city street.
This draft we soon returned to base:
"Please soften his unsmiling face."

The artist (as befits his role)
Replaced the knife with gospel scroll,
And gave his lips, with utmost guile,
The faintest apostolic smile.

Now set on high within his niche,
Safe from the rains which skies unleash,
He proudly from his height surveys
The passage of our common days.
The Chantry's shelter he'd disdain
For shelter from the driving rain.
But should the wind turn chill maybe
He'd like a friendly cup of tea?
The Lower Village Hall he sees
Is really rather on its knees.

But utmost praise he sure must sing
For those who plan some better thing.

Ted Walker's cattle he surveys,
Thinking maybe of far-off days
When herdsman's cry and school bell's chime
Remind us all it's milking time.
When Holder's horses thunder by
Does he perhaps avert his eye,
Lest he be tempted just to place
A fiver on the latest race?

What thoughts has he? Oh, none can tell
When Chubby chimes the old church bell.
But should these chimes disturb his rest
We know his smile is ever blessed.
No squabbling jackdaws from above
His gentle smile could e'er remove.
And if with sticks his pate they crown,
They know that he will never frown!
He, the Apostle, free from guile
Will sweetly on their antics smile.
Should Norman Slade when felling trees
Perchance disturb the martyr's peace,
Will he complain? Oh, surely not!
For martyrdom's his glorious lot.
Should bonfire smoke to him arise,
Will he not close his smarting eyes?
Oh no! For those who wink the eye
Aren't destined for eternity!

When bridal couples, hand in hand,
For wedding photos coyly stand,
He surely, too, with joyful zest
Will smile upon the couple blest.
And when at dusk the dark pines sway
With sighing at the close of day,
He from his niche secure the while
On one and all will warmly smile.

But most of all on sabbath day
When Failanders come here to pray,
We know his heart will surely thrill
With those who come to worship still.
For he, though sculpted here in stone,
Now dwells upon a heavenly throne,
And all the gathered saints shall feel
That he is with them as they kneel,
And we in one communion sing
High praises to our heavenly King.

Ring Out Wild Bells

(Easter Morning)

This is dedicated to church bell ringers.

Ring out wild bells, when sunrise eastward's flaming.
Ring out wild bells, in joyful glad accord.
Ring out wild bells, the Easter news proclaiming,
And tell the world that Jesus Christ is Lord!

Ring out wild bells, from ancient tower and steeple.
Ring out wild bells, amidst the earth's discord.
Ring out wild bells, and tell my troubled people
That he is risen! Yes, Jesus Christ is Lord!

Ring out wild bells, while people yet are sleeping.
Ring out wild bells, and loose the bounden cord.
Ring out wild bells, the world is in His keeping,
For he is risen! Yes, Jesus Christ is Lord!

Ring out wild bells, the silent world astounding.
Ring out wild bells, and tell the earth abroad.
Ring out wild bells, his Easter joy forth sounding.
Empty the tomb, for Jesus Christ is Lord!

Ring out wild bells, and let my people harken.
Ring out wild bells, as music heavenwards soared.
Ring out wild bells, no more shall sorrow darken
Their weary lives, for Jesus Christ is Lord!

Ring out wild bells, tell all the broken-hearted
Spring-time is here, the frozen earth has thawed.
The sun streams forth, the veil of sorrow's parted,
For he is risen! Yes, Jesus Christ is Lord!

Ring out wild bells, and let your glad rejoicing
Peal forth afresh, let music sound abroad!
Ring out wild bells, the Saviour's praises voicing,
For he is risen! Yes, Jesus Christ is Lord!

Ring out wild bells, at Easter sunrise dawning.
Ring out wild bells, in joyful glad accord.
Ring out wild bells, on this fair Easter morning,
Tell all the world that Jesus Christ is Lord!

Spring Awakening

Hidden all winter long beneath the frozen earth
The tiny seed imprisoned long cries out for birth.
The seed case holds the embryo in prison till
Warmth of spring sunshine causes it to swell.
Then secret seed-springs of the spirit soon shall break
Asunder and from deep within shall make
New life to blossom forth through pain.
This dying and this death is not in vain.

How many months I've lain imprisoned, lost,
And earthbound victim of this dark earth's frost.
Night of dark earth and hell of prisoned night
Shall break forth soon to greet the dawning light.
Pale yellow-white fleshed leaves within their case,
The embryonic seed cries out for space,
Space to erupt and burgeon forth from 'neath the earth.
Footfall of heavy clod and frost of winter's night
Has hid this lonely prisoner from the light.
Can he burst forth and fragile fronds unfold
Revealing there the beauty of a life untold?

Too much of duty's drudge, dull spirit killed,
Until the wonder of my Lord has filled
This poor starved seedling who once lay crushed.
And while in dark winter now the earth lies hushed,
Winter and frost have had their way,
The tiny seed cries out for light of day.

Wake, oh my soul! Imprisoned spirit heave!
The birth pangs of the spirit now shall cleave
Forth asunder from the bruised victim bound
And from the awful depths of frozen earth

There blossoms forth another kind of birth,
New birth of spirit working deep inside
The prison cell where once the seed of life died.

Yet even now the golden sunshine warms the earth,
The song thrush sings again 'midst signs of mirth.
The earthworm turns beneath the melting soil
Reminding us how days of patient toil
Have opened channels to the fresh clean air.
While old friend mole, he too has opened there
New crumbling earthworks by his ceaseless care.

Sunshine of springtime warms the frozen land
And tells me how my Lord so kindly planned
Seasons of fallow and a winter's rest.
How greatly with his goodness I am blessed,
Taught now in winter, much I've had to learn
Before this dark drear winter He could turn
Into a springtime, golden-glad and gay
With crocus, almond blossom and budding may.
Yes! Only golden sunshine melts the earthen frost
And warms the tiny seed that seemed cold lost.
And He, the Sun of Righteousness, shall rise
And shine upon you from the April skies.
He, too, who formed this prison's seed
Shall surely never fail to heed
The cries of those who, buried 'neath the earth,
Cry out for resurrection and new birth.
So now this frozen soul warmed by the sunshine sings
That "He is risen with healing in his wings.
All glory be to Him, great King of Kings!"

St Bartholomew (Failand) Amidst The Storm

**A small statue of the saint was placed in a niche and therefore
sheltered from the great storm of 1987.**

When tempest raged and wild storm lashed
Our ancient church, and pine trees crashed,
I wonder if our patron saint
Maybe was feeling rather faint?

Did he perchance amidst the blast
Cry out for help to those who passed,
And while the mighty thunders roll
Cling tightly to his Gospel scroll?

Did he not flinch amidst the gale?
Did fearful thoughts his soul assail?
Could he survive like mortal men
Amidst the howling gale force ten?

Perched up aloft, within his niche,
Did he his billowing cassock hitch
Up just one notch, in case the breeze
Should chill the apostolic knees?

Oh no! Within his niche secure
His countenance composed, demure,
Unruffled, smiles within the storm
With noble brow and saintly form.

While lesser mortals trembling quake,
He rock-like stands, no storm can shake
This saint of old who perched on high
Has surely heard our anguished cry.

No sign of stress or strain shows he,
His brow unfurrowed yet shall be.
Secure within his niche the while
Looks down with beatific smile.

Custodian of our Church, secure
Within his Rock, he will endure
Whatever stormy blasts assail,
His life now hid within the veil.

Untroubled there within his niche
He surely would us mortals teach
That we within the Rock must hide
And shelter in the Saviour's side.

The Burning Bush

Exodus 3 (1-9)

This extraordinary theophany (appearance of God) describes an awesome revelation to Moses after he was commanded to lead the children of Israel out of captivity in Egypt, a task for which he felt totally unprepared.

When Moses in the wilderness did keep
The flock of Jethro, priest of Midian's sheep,
There at a time of Israel's bondage dire
The Lord appeared in bush with flame of fire.
And Moses, seeing what he least presumed,
The bush was burning, yet was not consumed.
And Moses said, "I'll turn aside and see
The meaning of this awesome mystery."
And then from 'midst the bush a voice there came,
The Lord God calling Moses by his name.
And he in awe before such majesty
Cried out in terror, "Here am I."
The Lord God said, "Do not come nigh,
Put off your shoes and trembling look around.
The place on which you stand is holy ground.
I am the God of Abraham, Isaac, and the God
Of Jacob, who this way have trod."
And Moses, sore afraid, then hid his face,
Fearful of seeing Him in such a place.
But now the Lord God spoke in living tones:
"I now have seen and heard my people's groans,
I know their bondage and their suffering.
Salvation to my people now I'll bring,
Out of Egypt, Pharaoh's cruel hand,
And lead you to a broad and spacious land.
A land where milk and sweetest honey flow,
A land to which you now shall surely go,

There to deliver, set my people free
From Pharaoh's yoke and cruel slavery.
Come, I will send you now to Egypt's King
And great delivrance to my people bring."

But Moses said to God, "O, who am I
To bring thy people out of slavery?"
The Lord God said, "I'll be with you, and this the sign
That I have sent you, this the seal divine:
When out of Egypt you and the people've trod
Here on this mountain you shall worship God!"

The Ransomed Of The Lord Return With Joy

(Isaiah 35 paraphrase)

The wilderness and dry land sings
As each becomes the place of springs
Where fountains play and streamlets flow
And fairest flowers shall freely grow.
Gold crocuses and Sharon's rose
Whose mystic petals each disclose
The beauty of the Son of God
Who once himself this desert trod.

The hills of Lebanon shall shine
With glory of His light divine,
And he who looks on high shall see
Mount Carmel clothed with majesty.
The glory of the Lord shall be
Revealed in awesome purity.
To those who come with trembling knee
He says, "Fear not for I am He
Who by my spirit set you free.
Reach out all you who trembling stand
And take my loving nail-pierced hand.
To those I say of fearful heart,
I am your God, there is no part
For craven fear and wond'rings vain,
I am your God who comes to reign!"

Then blind eyes shall be opened wide
As He the bridegroom greets the bride.
Deaf ears unstopped shall hear His voice
And hearing Him their hearts rejoice!
With joy the loosened tongues shall sing
Fresh praises to their heavenly King.

The wilderness and dry land sings
As each becomes a place of springs.
The burning sand becomes a pool
Of limpid waters, crystal cool.
The haunt of jackals changed by grace
Shall now be called a resting place.
Dry grass becomes fresh green and lush
With swaying reed and piping rush.
A highway He has builded there,
A holy way, and none shall dare
To tread upon that holy ground
Except the ransomed of the Lord who've found
The living way, as sons of God:
Redemption in the Saviour's blood.
No prowling lion or ravenous beast
Shall there molest the very least
Of all God's children as they tread
The pilgrim's way that he has led.

Then all the world shall greet this dawn,
The ransomed of the Lord return
Upon the loved and ancient ways
To Zion, singing loud his praise.
For lo! He reigns the King of Kings
Now risen with healing in his wings.
Sorrow and sighing flee away
Like desert mists at break of day.
Their heads raised high, each pilgrim sings
"All glory to the King of Kings".

Epiphany: The Wise Men's Offering

See how they greet Him, newborn infant King,
See how they kneel, and costliest treasures bring.
See how they offer gifts from hearts adoring,
Raptured in silence while the angels sing,
"Glory to God in the highest".
Yet now they humbly kneel
On earth's hard floor, with joyful hearts exulting,
Silent in adoration, their lowly offering.

Gold for the child, His glorious kingship telling,
And frankinscense for Him as Son of God.
Myrrh for the Saviour's last anointing,
Humbly they kneel upon the earthen sod,
Kneel in the stable where the babe lies sleeping,
Straw for his bed and oxen's breath to warm,
Safe in the arms of Mary's gentle keeping.
Here they discern the Saviour's tiny form.
Here, in the shadows, Joseph quietly watches
Over the mother and her infant child.
Is he aware of God's eternal purpose,
One day within that life to be fulfilled?
Is he aware that one day his dear mother
Shall weep with Him in hour of bitter loss?
Is he aware that those he once called 'brother'
Shall turn on Him and nail Him to a cross?
Does He, asleep now in the manger,
Stir in the small hours as the shadows play
And realise here, so far away from danger,
That all the world will one day Him obey?
Does He, with tiny hands outstretching,
Reaching for comfort at dear Mary's breast,
Know that upon a cross He too will offer comfort

To His dear mother and the apostle blest?
Does He but know, so tiny, weak and helpless
Here in the manger filled with hay,
That, oh, the world He came to is so heartless,
And Him the Son of God they'll do away?

Did they the Magi, child adoring,
(Breathless in worship now we see them kneel),
Did they, the Wise Men, in their hearts adoring,
Guess for a moment what this child would feel?
Cross of harsh oak and bitter tongues deriding,
Pierce of cruel nails, as for His blood they cry,
"We have no king but Caesar; crucify Him!"
And so the King of Glory goes His way.

Hushed in the stable now in silent worship
See how they kneel upon the earthen sod.
Do they perceive, within that infant form reclining,
He who is Saviour, King and Son of God?

To Anne and Jonathan

**A bouquet of flowers for Anne and Jonathan on their engagement,
Lee Abbey, 31 May 1958**

See, here's campion, culled from the hedgerow wild,
Soft to proclaim for each thy child,
With warm pink blush of love
The rose breathed flame of His own giving.
Nestled within, the wild hedge parsley's tiny flower
Shall tell His purity, and at each hour
Clear bluebells ring in sun or shower
And joy proclaim, the Saviour's dower.
Trefoil, encircling all, shall tell of three:
Faith, hope and love, and these agree
For they are thine and these are thine
Who at thy shrine have knelt and there received
What love's strange pattern weaved.
His mystic gift, and there adored
In Him as one, their Lord.
Here, too, the may shall evermore rejoice
From blossomed spray and sing, one heart and voice,
"God bless you both."

And we, as children of one family,
Shall wrap you round with moss of love and prayer.
His care, best gardener of all,
Shall tend and keep you fair
And fresh as wild spring flowers
E'er grown in Easter garden.

The Moonlit Lake (St Julian's)

This poem was inspired when the author, while staying at the retreat house at Coolham near Horsham as a guest, heard the bark of a fox and the scream of startled moorhens and coots.

Cold sparkles frost tonight,
Ghost-like the lake
Dreams in the moonlight.
Creatures awake.
Rustle of silver sedge,
Splash by the weir,
Fox slinks by water's edge,
Ducks freeze for fear.
Startled, a water-hen
'Quirrups' then flies,
Hectic wings water beat
In moonlight surprise.

Swans sail serenely,
Ghost-like, unreal.
Phantoms of dream lake
Like Odette/Odile,
Proudly as galleons
They glide o'er the mere,
Silver-plumed dalliance
Like princess and peer.
He prince of these waters,
She safe in his wake,
Enchanted have brought us
To gaze at their lake.

Then fox-startled geese
Asleep on the isle

Sharp shatter the peace
Of this dreamy moonwhile.
Fox-leap in frost weather
As water hens scream,
Then flurry of feather
And crimsoned the stream,
As fox-fang in anger
Sinks deep in the bird,
And owl cry of danger
O'er iced waters heard.

Then rustle by hedgerow
And Reynard is gone,
And bloodstained the sedge shows
Where murder was done.
Frost silvered ferns
At these night horrors quake,
Then silence returns
To the frost sparkling lake.
At rush-root the bream
And the roach and the chub
Shudder 'midst moon-dream
Asleep on the mud.

Now scurry the dark clouds
'Cross the star-studded sky,
Death-drawn like the dark shrouds
Where iced waters lie.
The night air bites keenly,
Now calm lies the deep
As swans sail serenely
The lake falls asleep.
As prince with his princess
Their 'pas de deux' make,
So they glide in the moonlight
O'er sleeping Swan Lake.

The Sun

*This is my earliest extant poem written at the age of 9 for 'The Badger',
the school magazine of The Downs School, a lovely Quaker school at
Colwall near Great Malvern in Worcestershire.*

The sun is glorious,
The sun has a fiery glow.
How large and hot it is,
Never a soul did know.

The sun is glorious,
It brightens up the gloom.
It makes each little bud
Send forth its pretty bloom.

The sun is glorious,
It shines right from the sky.
Right from its bed of space
In heights so very high.

HUMOROUS VERSE

As You Were, Chaps

A fatal mis-print at Eaton Hall, Chester.
(With apologies to His Grace, the Duke)

Eaton Hall, near Chester, is the hereditary seat of the Dukes of Westminster. It was for some years after the second world war an officer training school for young National Servicemen. The poem was inspired by a fatal misprint in the invitation to a service of dedication where the word 'plague' was mistakenly printed instead of 'plaque'

Your letter dated August 10
Has rather shocked us older men
Who, forty summers past, recall
Those golden days at Eaton Hall.
Our memories now though rather vague
Can scarce recall an army plague!

Did we not come as raw recruits
And learn to spit and polish boots,
And, courtesy of ducal grace,
Make there awhile our dwelling place?

Hounded by tyrants Copp or Lynch
We learned quite quickly not to flinch
When pace-sticks raked our shining boots,
We really didn't care two hoots.
Put on a charge, we'd bravely smile
When marched 'up office' by Sergeant Pile.

And should we fail our M.K.5
We could repair to some good dive
In Chester where with trilbys (brown)
We'd have a night out on the town.
Quaintways we loved and Clements too,
Yet feared we much an R.T.U.

With Colonel Gibbs (and later Nott)
We really learned an awful lot,
Though Queens and Worcesters we avowed
Would never make us brave lads cowed.

Chastised, corrected, humbled, abased,
Across parade grounds we were chased
By Sergeant Majors whom we knew full well
Could make our lives one living hell!

Route marches, full-kit, at the double
Would leave us like a heap of rubble.
Yet showered, refreshed by cook-house tea,
We'd wander quietly by the Dee.

Some lucky lads I do recall
Were billeted inside the Hall,
While others, undeserving muts,
Were stuck outside in Nissen huts!

At Battle Camp (Okehampton, Devon)
We came so near to hell or heaven.
Yet 'neath the eye of Captain Ward
Our mortal destiny's assured.

Four months we sweated hard and long,
And managed still a marching song,
Till with the C.O's kind permission
We each received the King's commission.

And then (does memory now forget?)
Our names were in the Court Gazette.
As proudly we in service dress
And Sam Browne clad, first joined the Mess.

Now forty summers past have fled
And some old comrades we fear dead.
Yet we tonight can still recall
Those golden days at Eaton Hall.

That ancient pile, alas, has gone,
Yet still the clock tower lingers on.
And R.S.M. good Desmond Lynch:
We think you've scarcely shrunk an inch!

And you, sir, erstwhile Captain Ward
Of Welsh Guards fame, can well afford
To smile upon this motley band
Who trembled once at your command.

And you, Sir Charles, fresh from the Rhine
Have come amongst us here to dine,
As we old veterans now recall
Those far off days at Eaton Hall.

But pray, good sirs, lest you mistook
The wishes of the noble Duke,
Our Dinner Secretary's strayed.
One vital letter he mislaid:
In Standing Orders rather vague
Insert one 'plaque', delete one 'plague'!

In Reply To The Editors' Termly Circular

This was written for the Sherburnian Magazine in 1949 in response to an urgent plea for contributions.

I hope this contribution
Will be part of the solution
To the doleful lack of writing in your rag.
Tho' poor in execution
I will call this retribution
For my previous lack of interest in the Mag.
But the truth is I've been dreaming
While your editors were screaming
At the apathy and malaise of the School.
And while my brain is teeming
I am sure that you'll be beaming
At the unaspiring efforts of a fool.

When A Knight Won His Spurs

To The Rev Peter Wills, MA, MFH

This is a humorous 'send up' of a great friend of mine, partially true and partially fictional.

At The Horseman's Service

Proud prelate who now mounted stands,
A thousand fillies' lives commands.
To wind and rain impervious he,
Seated on high in majesty
Upon his Arab stallion proud,
Gazing benignly on the crowd.
Booted and spurred, be-cassocked he
Is really quite a sight to see.
No filly moves 'midst this concourse,
Peter is Master of the Horse.

Rank upon rank they gathered there,
Stallion and gelding, filly and mare,
As he with lordly eye surveys
The passage of their common days.
And silent they (I know not how)
Their equine heads in reverence bow.
For each who's come must know perforce
'Tis Peter, Master of the Horse.

And every eye is fixed on he
Who's seated now in majesty.)
"The time has come for stirrup cup.

So charge your glasses, gentles all,
Before I from my horse do fall."
Hip flask he takes from cassock wide
And calls a toast for all who ride.
"Good cheer, kind friends, to one and all.
Here's to all creatures, great and small!"
And gladly they each raise the glass
Before this mighty throng shall pass.
"And here's to Peter who, of course,
We know is Master of the Horse."

Flax Bourton's Rector, perched on high,
Wipes back a tear from bloodshot eye.
"My friends", quoth he, "On this great day
You've nobly come, a vast array,
And 'ere this mighty downpour's ceased
Let's raise a glass to man and beast.
So charge your cups good gentles all,
Methinks The Jubilee doth call.
Ring out the old! Ring in the new!
With 'Gone Away' and 'View Halloo'!"

So Peter perched on stallion proud
Smiles now benignly on the crowd.
"Good riders all, I now decree
We shall repair to Jubilee."
With sudden cry his steed he turns
And leads the chase, all caution spurns,
And with a shout that rends the skies
Rides off to gain the glittering prize.

Here sadly now the story ends,
A curtain on the scene descends.
Dear Peter from his steed did fall,
An ambulance at once they'd call.
Police came, too, as you surmised
And had him promptly breathalysed.
"Above the limit!" they decreed,
And so he's banished from his steed.
No more the chase and stirrup cup,

For Pete the hunt is surely up.
And on the Rectory gate (they say)
Hangs a sad notice: 'Gone Away'!

The moral of this tale is clear:
To 'drink and drive' will cost you dear.
To all who run this earthly course,
You must be Master of your Horse!

Steam Days

It is very probable that David Howell and I both looked over the same railway bridge near Primrose Hill in the mid-1930s. David, himself a keen railway buff in later years, was to become my very dear friend and colleague at the Crowhurst Home for Christian Healing near Battle in East Sussex. There is, in the last line, a play on words, "Howell with Payne"!

In days of by-gone steam perchance
I from my childhood pram would glance
And there observe, at Primrose Hill,
Those giants of the track who still
With shining hulk and brass a-gleam
Would there emit huge clouds of steam.
With 'huff and puff' it reached the skies
At Camden Town or Kensal Rise.
My childish ears would gladly thrill
At piercing whistle, clear and shrill.
With lumbering gait they would slow down
Approaching near to Camden Town.
I'd squeeze my head between the bars
Of that old bridge, and gaze for hours
There to behold my childhood dream,
The scent and sight and sound of steam.

My mother oft would gently say,
"I think it's time we went away."
But I'd reply with anguished pain,
"Oh, can't we stay for one more train?"

So there we were, young 'loco' spies,
Near Camden Town or Kensal Rise.
But war-time came with dread bomb-blast,
A veil that's made those memories seem
Like some imagined childhood dream.

And now some fifty years have passed
Since we would watch them, slow and fast.
Maybe it's time we both went back
To gaze upon the ancient track.
No puff of steam or whistle shrill
Our middle-aged ears would thrill.
We'd *howl* with *pain* when we espied
The ancient line electrified!

(To David Howell *from David* Payne*!)*

Resurgam

This was written for a dear friend of mine who is (happily) still with us.

Dear Father John, we're glad to learn
That you have taken now a turn
For the better, for we feared
Perhaps that you had disappeared
Beneath the bedclothes and, poor thing,
Had even heard the angels sing.
Indeed the doctor gravely said
"I think perhaps he may be dead."
Such pallor on your noble brow,
He really rather wondered how
You'd last the night. But you contrived
To do just this, and thus survived
To tell the tale as morning dawned,
The medics grim prognosis scorned,
Confounding the physician who
Had said his last fair fond "Adieu".
Your temperature had soared on high
Your brow was hot, your palate dry.
The stabbing headache and the cough
Had left you feeling pretty rough,
And, like old Falstaff (scanning yields),
You'd been 'a'babbling of green fields'.
But Naomi's devoted skill
Hath succoured you when gravely ill.
The soothing hand and tender touch
Applied by your esteemed Old Dutch,
As she with easeful skill and grace
Smiled on your beatific face.
And though content within your bed
The fever and the ague fled!
So praise the Lord! And bless your wife,
You've entered 'resurrection life'!

Pride Comes Before A Fall

To George

This is a fanciful embroidering of a true incident.

Clad in pyjamas and a dressing gown
George goes to feed the swans upon the lawn.
Like gallant Siegfried in 'Swan Lake'
Across the dewy sward himself doth take.
A shadowy figure amidst the mist
At the break of dawn makes solemn tryst.
And, like Nureyev, doth proudly stand
And offer bread from his most bounteous hand.

Regal he stands, a handsome prince
(Yet that which follows will make you wince).
The cob, sans warning, takes sudden fright,
Makes a vicious pass, George turns in fright.
Alas, too late! His 'flip-flops' skid and disappear
And George falls down, upon his rear.
A cry goes up, "Oh, help! Fair Susan come
And haul me up. I've landed on my bum!"

Fair Susan hears (for sleep has fled)
And leaps up smartly from the bridal bed.
"Oh, George! My gallant prince so dear,
Why are you lying on your rear?"
Too late! The damage has been done!
The neighbours saw it all – what fun!
And on video camera, no mistake,
Recorded one more excerpt from 'Swan Lake'.
'The Prince's Fall', they call it. What a treat!
It'll soon be released: the Odeon at Fleet.

And George, now chastened by the fall
Has gone off swans – I'm not surprised at all!

Requiem For Roland Rat

A child's toy

The cat, Freya by name, owned by my daughter Alison has recently died.
Roland Rat, with a huge muzzle, can scarcely be called other than very ugly!

H ere lies the body of Roland Rat
Who pushed his luck with a certain cat
Just a shade too far (and paid the price).
What follows now is <u>not</u> very nice!

He worried her day and night until
She lost all patience and went for the kill.
Upon our Roly did Freya leap,
And Roly winced as her teeth bit deep.

He danced and he reared, but all in vain,
His spinal column was severed in twain.
As the blood flowed forth he was heard to mutter,
"I should have stuck to bread and butter!"

With that he drew his final breath
And Roland died an untimely death.
The vetinr'y said 'twas natural causes,
But we knew well 'twas Freya's pawsies!

So here he lies on New Year's Day,
And rigor mortis has come to stay.
As Roland's life has come to a close
He lies here cold, in a state of repose.

And you who have travelled from warmer climes
May hear the church bells' mournful chimes.
A priest has been summoned to offer 'stat',
A requiem for Roland Rat.

The moral of the tale cannot be missed:
A rat and a cat just <u>can't</u> co-exist!

Owed To An English Rose

To Barbara Watt, Lee Abbey, N. Devon, 1958

This was written to the kind 'housebod' who cleaned my 'horsebox' at Lee Abbey when it was in terrible disorder!

My horsebox lay all in disorder
Books, bedclothes and boots all awry.
A bachelor's bedlam, a bear den,
Beastlier far than a piggy-wig's sty.

The 'housebod' who strove to amend this
Tried beseeching and pleading – in vain,
For the brute beast who lived in such squalor
Was an ignorant poultryman – Payne!

Though she shamed him by singing the praises
Of the horsebox all housebods adored,
He confessed he was not such a master
Of matters domestic as Ward.

"If only", he said, "they'd provide us
With a feminine touch (such as flowers)
Why, of course we'd be tidy as Guiders
And we'd sweep, spit and polish all hours."

Such remarks he'd only made lightly,
('Twas his wont to be flippant and gay).
But it's clear that the lady that heard them
Must have taken his words t'other way.

For on his return in the evening,
Just ready for ten minutes' doze,
He opened the door of his horsebox
And there stood a fair English rose!

Now this fellah had heard about flowers,
(Though he'd not met Miss Constance Spry).
But to see that there rose all a'bloomin –
Well, it soon brought a tear to his eye.

He'd heard about flowers on birthdays,
(He had often picked wallflowers for Mum).
But the Warden had told him in P.R.s,
"For the girls, flowers is <u>out</u>. Sorry, chum!"

But he'd added, "In cases of sickness
Or other extremes, as you knows,
Well, of course, you can give aspidistras,
Or even a fair English Rose!

So the poultryman's cherished that flower,
He thinks it's the luvliest bloom.
And he promises once every hour
<u>Some</u> day he'll sweep the – room!

Ode To An Unknown Community Bachelor, Lee Abbey, 1958

This was written about a hole, some six feet by two feet, which David Barrett, plumber and handyman at the Lee Abbey Community in North Devon, had dug. It contains a line which is a parody on 'Walk The Barratt Way', a slogan for the well-known Northampton shoemakers.

N. Devon, 1958

Here lies the body of poor honest Joe,
Who never learned to wash or iron or mend or even sew.
He joined the Community, a handsome lad,
Tall, spruce and dapper, and so nicely clad.
He wore nylon panties and a big string vest
With lots and lots of holies (for the hairs upon his chest).
His Mummy told him, "Darling, if washing hard you find,
Just ask those lovely sisters, I am sure that they'll be kind.
But his sisters never offered (they didn't care a stitch),
They simply muttered, "Drip dry", and left him in the ditch.
His undies changed from Persil white to sombre shades of grey,
His shirties fell to pieces and his socks just crept away.
He tried Omo, Daz and Persil, and many more beside,
He telegrammed his parents saying, "Mother, send us Tide."
But he never learned to wash, or iron, or mend or even sew,
And I'm so very, very sad to tell this tale of woe.
His sisters, they scorned him, for despite an air of ease
They confessed he reminded them of Gorgonzola cheese.
At last he took to bed, wearing not a single stitch.
They diagnosed 'exposure' and a kind of 'seven year itch'.
The nurse, she fetched the doctor, but too late for he had died,
And his dying words to Geoffrey were, "No flowers, please, soap and Tide."
They laid him to his rest, in the yard just by the drain,
And I fear that he will never walk the Barrett way again!
And you, good gentle sisters, as you read this sad, sad page,
Will you pray now for the coming of the golden Drip Dry Age?

Harping On

Tyntesfield is a large country estate between Bristol and Clevedon, formerly belonging to Lord Wraxall and now the property of the National Trust. Richard Hook was an employee of the late Lord Wraxall and this poem is a fictitious account of his attempt to learn the harp.

When night-time falls at old Home Farm
And all around 'tis dark,
Then music calm our ears doth charm,
'Tis Richard at his harp!

When cattle in the meadows lie
So peaceful in the park,
Angelic music's heard on high,
'Tis Richard at his harp!

Should children from deep slumber wake
Their youthful ears so sharp,
Then they with fear and terror quake,
'Tis Richard at his harp!

When all around there's not a sound,
Nor e'en the foxes bark,
For refuge they have gone to ground
For fear of Richard's harp!

When wandering bats a-flitter round
Keen ears their passage mark.
And birds on wing hear one loud 'ping',
'Tis Richard at his harp!

When fairest Sal hath gone to bed
Wearied at close of day
With awful dread she holds her head
'Tis Richard on his harp!

When neighbours call to voice complaint
(They're not the ones to carp),
With one accord they say "M'Lord
'Tis Richard on his harp."

When good Lord Wraxall lies awake
He is inclined to bark
As he his lordly head doth shake,
"'Tis Richard at his harp!"

When Raymond and his Betty fair
Exhausted by this lark,
Will they not say at close of day,
"'Tis Richard at his harp!"

And so the whole of Tyntesfield knows
(Their ears are really sharp)
That when 'The Sound of Music' grows,
'Tis Richard at his harp!

They ring His Lordship, all in vain,
(He's not the one to carp),
As they in pain now all complain
Of Richard at his harp!

Fair Sal hath lost her youthful bloom,
She cries out in the dark,
She's even had to change her room
For Richard and his harp!

And so at last the music dies,
Peace reigns in old Home Farm,
Richard's ascended to the skies,
The angel hosts to charm!

And so my harping tale is told,
The great Archangel sings,
"That bloomin' harp can now be sold,
Our Richard's got his wings!"

Girl In A Whirl

Edna Madgwick, Lee Abbey, 1958

This was written at Lee Abbey, N. Devon, when Edna Madgwick, a fellow community member, was seen practising the (then) current 'hula hoop' craze.

Our Ed's quite a girl for the hula,
You should see her fair twirling it round.
While she kicks and she sways and she wiggles,
Oh, she's 'being herself' I'll be bound!

She hulas, we think, in the lunch hour,
(Walled garden is probably the spot),
And 'tis commonly known that the wallflowers
Protest she is hotter than hot.

She has vied with the keenest of youngsters,
(Our Shirls and our Audrey and more),
And it's whispered her waistline's so tiny
Next season she'll 'show' for Dior.

The hula has brought liberation
To Edna and many besides,
And it's rumoured she'll play at the Palais,
(Dear reader, no quips or asides!)

She has bought, says the grapevine, new longpants
Of tartan the gayest of gay,
But we'll search all in vain for her waistline,
For it's feared that she's 'waisted' away.

Now the moral, dear girls, is quite obvious,
Too long you have sat on the shelf.
Buy a sweater, a hoop and some longpants,
And jolly well BE YOUR OWN SELF!

Get On Parade

This is partially fictional but based on fact. It begins humorously but ends seriously.

The General (I have heard it said)
Did neither sleep nor go to bed
For many weeks before the day
When wedding bells were due to play.

The General, or C.R.A.,
Unconsciously began to play
The role he once (oh, please don't laugh!)
Had occupied as Chief of Staff.
The 'phone lines hummed for many hours
To Mary D who's O/C Flowers.
Each pedestal and dainty spray
Was then discussed by night and day,
Till she begain to wonder why
She'd not been christened Constance Spry!
The Verger said, "Ahem! Ahem!
Another call from Mrs M!"

The General paced out the aisle
Of our dear church, that ancient pile,
Just to be sure the ushers knew
The right procedure to pursue.
He quietly then sussed out the pews
And measured each lest he should lose
One single inch of space, because
That would be deemed a fatal loss.
"Nor must a guest be hidden away
Behind a pillar", he did say.
Those pillars he did sadly rue,
Which would obstruct the people's view.

The rood screen, too, he oft surveyed
Lest it might hinder the parade
Who, as they marched from nave to choir,
Might miss the order, "Open fire!"

The great day came (as you will glean),
The General surveyed the scene
And then with smiling face aglow
Agreed the chaps had made a splendid show!
"Full decorations shall be given
To all who valiantly have striven.
The Verger, cleaner, Mary know,
They may receive a D.S.O.
And others who worked hard (in patches)
May well be Mentioned in Dispatches."
The Chief of Staff (in no great hurry)
Arrived, on time, with Mrs Curry,
And there the front pew occupied,
Awaiting bridegroom and the bride.
A bugle sounds! The organ played
A fanfare (or a fusillade?).
Twelve guns salute! 'Midst wild alarms
The order's given to "PREE-SENT ARMS!"
The door swings wide and in there spills
The ample frame of Father Wills,
His tonsured head all neatly shorn
And medal ribbons (somewhat worn).
The chaps leap up, the organ played
For this the bridal cavalcade.
Then up the aisle, yes, side by side,
There comes the bridegroom and the bride.
And bridesmaids fair, with flower sticks gripped
Behind the couple blithely tripped.

The service, lasting scarce one hour,
Is filled with joy and led by choir,
While Father Wills, the Acting Padre,
Briefly exhorts this noble cadre:
"Well, chaps, as you must surely know,

This is a really first class show.
And for the bridegroom and the bride,
Who occupy the place of pride,
I ask you now to rise and stand
And loudly clap with upraised hand."

Later the couple walk to kneel
Before the altar, and we feel
The hand of God upon them laid
As each their promises have made.
And they, the kneeling couple, know
That God has blessed them as they go.
And so on this most happy day
We kneel with them and humbly pray
That on this bridal couple blessed
The hand of God may ever rest.

Fortune Fades

This is a humorous and entirely fictitious caricature of a regular visitor to my aunt in North London.

While Cuthbert doth my aunt beguile,
Couched there on beds of camomile,
Fortune on him shall surely smile,
He's scented my Clark's shares!

While he like Romeo doth pursue
His Juliet (aged eighty-two),
He knows she's worth a bob or two
Made up of Clark's Shoes shares.

Sure as the breaking of the dawn
He calls at ten each Friday morn.
What secret hopes in him are born
Of hands on Clark's Shoes shares?

With dulcet tone and soothing voice
He offers her a tempting choice,
And whispers in her ear, "Dear Joyce,
I'm after your Clark's shares!"

They say with age that love grows cold
Yet I perceive he grows more bold,
He knows at last he's striking gold
Made up of Clark's Shoes shares.

Sweet nothings whispers he perchance
(I fear he leads her quite a dance!)
Pursuing my inheritance
Made up of Clark's Shoes shares!

While Cuthbert plies his ancient charms
Her fevered brow he gently calms,
And that my troubled soul alarms,
He's after my Clark's shares!

We thought perchance that Nether Street
Might once be ours, a thought so sweet,
But now he's kneeling at her feet
The vision disappears!

Yes, life has changed at '129'
Since two young hearts did intertwine.
My fortune's frankly on the line
And I am full of fears.

With dulcet tone he doth beguile,
My aunt he knows is worth a pile.
On him the sun shall surely smile,
My fortune disappears!

He gentle Quaker, pacifist,
My ageing aunt hath fondly kissed.
No opportunities he's missed
Of poaching my Clark's shares!

There on the sofa in his arms
She soon succumbs to all his charms
And dishes out with open palms
Too many of my shares!

But things are coming to the crunch:
He stays on now for Friday lunch
And deep within I have a hunch
He's after my Clark's shares!

Too late I fear, he's run amok
And found my aunt a sitting duck.
So now, my lads, we're out of luck,
There'll be no Clark's Shoes shares!

She was a Street girl we know well,
Oh, what a story she could tell,
But now the Clark's shares she must sell
To pay for his arrears!

Gone my illusions, the winter's past,
Cuthbert has moved just a shade too fast
And I fear we shall feel the icy blast –
It's goodbye to my Clark's shares.

For we who are left the bell doth toll,
We'll spend our days upon the dole,
For Clark's inheritance is up the pole
And we are left in tears!

Fall From Grace

This was sent to Archbishop Robert Runcie after he fell in an attic while collecting suitcases before a lecture tour to Australia.

D ear Doctor, I am sad to read
You fell from grace. Did you not heed
The warnings of your wife who oft
Said, "Robert, climbing in the loft
Is not a thing you ought to do
When you're approaching seventy-two"?
(Not every cleric's fall from grace
Came in pursuit of one suitcase!)
Did you perchance, the friend of kings,
Aspire too much to higher things,
And from your lofty perch did call,
"There's one above who knoweth all"?
And so I fear the ladder slipped,
Or was it that your footstep tripped?
And with a landing none too soft
You fell from grace, out of the loft.
Your bold ascent made all in vain,
You lay there helpless, wracked with pain,
And at the feet of Rosalind
Confessed that you indeed had sinned.
And now your frame and crutches mastered
You return home – plastered.
Your lecture tour, alas, deferred
The waiting crowds we know have heard
Your script has now been re-arranged
The title of your talk is changed.
No more Bronowski-like (won't scan)
Will you exalt 'The Ascent of Man',
But last of the primates now will call
"Some Reflections on the Fall".

Coxes In Boxes

I gathered some Coxes apples from the royal orchards near Sandringham.

These apples come by royal decree,
A present from Her Majesty
Who, wandring through her orchards, saw
These golden Coxes, ripe to store,
And thought perchance (a sudden whim)
That they be right for Sue and Tim.
And so they come by royal command,
Untouched of course by human hand.

Her ancestor, good Henry V,
(I'm sad to say he's not alive)
Received a gift from France of old
Of something rather less than gold:
A cheeky gift which now appals –
A box of second-hand tennis balls,
Sent by the King of France' command,
Delivered by the Dauphin's hand.
This drove the noble good King Harry
Into a really frightful fury.
So, reck'ning a lesson should be taught,
He whopped the French at Agincourt.

But I digress, this royal box
Is filled instead with ripening Cox.
The royal physician oft hath said,
"Take one before you go to bed!"

And so they come, just right for eating,
With the most cordial Royal greeting.

Elizabeth R

Come On, The Saints!

A poem inspired by reading in the Church Press the announcement
of the appointment of The Rev. John Perry, Warden of Lee Abbey,
to be Bishop of Southampton, and The Ven. Paul Barber, Archdeacon of
Surrey, to be Bishop of Northampton. NorthamptonRFC and
Southampton FC are both nicknamed 'The Saints'.

On reading my Church Press today
I learned of two good priests who say
They've been called (oh, what a wrench)
To sit upon the Bishops' bench.

John to Southampton, Paul to North,
From east and west their sound goes forth,
But do they know, both John and Paul,
The common nature of their call?

John to The Dell is summoned now,
And Paul to Franklyns Gardens. How
The good Lord hearing their complaints
Has called them both to join the Saints!

Clad in fine purple they will root
For sinners who put in the boot,
Averting eyes from human taints
With holy cries, "Come on, the Saints!"

With mitred head and upraised hands
We see them glorious in the stands,
Exhorting those whose spirit faints,
Their cry goes up, "Come on, the Saints!"

No hooligan durst haunt The Dell
For fear he be condemned to hell.
While he who errs at Franklyns Gardens
May plead in vain for Bishop's pardons.

If at The Dell it's one-nil down,
Then Bishop John will surely frown
And freed from Lee Abbey's restraints
Will cry aloud, "Come on, the Saints!"

At Franklyns Gardens Bishop Paul
May spot the crooked line-out ball.
And yet (despite the ref's complaints)
Still yell aloud, "Come on, the Saints!"

And if the reffy's word seems hard
Maybe they'll show a purple card,
Clutching their pect'ral cross (or rattle)
Exhorting saints to join the battle!

And when the game is lost or won
And muddied Saints their duty done,
The Bishop's train with no constraints
Will cry aloud, "Well played, the Saints!"

And so to Hamptons (South and North)
We know that they will journey forth,
Inspired by sainthood's glorious vision:
Promotion to the First Division!

The Lady Isobelle

This was the name of the vessel (one of the original Dunkirk Little Ships) to whom I dedicated this poem just after Valentine's Day.

I've met a Lady of such charms
She fills my soul with wild alarms.
I've lain but once within her arms,
Sweet Lady Isobelle.

Moored up beside the 'Amsel', she
My heart beguiled, 'tis plain to see,
And hence this haunting eulogy
To Lady Isobelle.

Graceful in line, her beauty such
I dare not tell my dear old Dutch
How I do love her very much,
The Lady Isobelle.

Though veterans both of sixty years
She's filled my heart with, oh, such fears,
And writing this I'm moved to tears
For love of Isobelle.

Her bodywork resplendent now,
Revarnished she from stern to prow,
Her magic works – I know not how –
The Lady Isobelle.

As swans serene glide up the river
She sets my youthful heart a-quiver,
And I can only shake and shiver
For love of Isobelle

Her paintwork shining in the sun,
The course of true love now has run
And she much damage now hath done,
Alas! Fair Isobelle.

Such foolish thoughts I once forswore,
But I am ready – well – for more.
This lovely Lady I adore!
The Lady Isobelle.

The waves her shapely form caress,
And now aloud I do confess
I'm suffering with signs of stress
Brought on by Isobelle.

Veteran indeed of far Dunkirk,
Her duty she did never shirk.
Strange fears within my heart do lurk
When I see Isobelle.

Young Boney met his Waterloo,
Is this the day that I shall rue
And earn a mention in 'Who's Who',
Yes, me and lovely Isobelle?

Like Josephine in Boney's arms
My soul is filled with wild alarms,
For I've succumbed to all her charms,
The Lady Isobelle.

They say with age we wiser get –
I've never met an old fool yet
Immune to Cupid's crafty net,
It's thus with Isobelle.

What shall we do in such a state,
Can we turn back? Is it too late?
Do we detect the hand of Fate,
Me and my Isobelle?

Shall we launch out and risking all
Answer the tideway's silent call?
Who knows what ventures might befall
Both me and Isobelle?

Shall we like Ulysses of old
Sail off once more on ventures bold
And find afar our 'cloth of gold'?
Who knows, fair Isobelle?

Such fantasies must flee away,
Vanquished in Finchley I must stay.
We'll meet again some happy day,
My Lady Isobelle!

To Our Well-Beloved Canon Bal(dock)

This was written on his promotion to be a Canon.

Martin, I hear you're canonised!
And I for one am not surprised.
As one who knew you long ago
And watched the sapling curate grow
Into full manhood – six feet four –
We little guessed what lay in store!

Your mighty exploits we recall
On t'cricket field with bat and ball,
And how the opposition quailed
Whom you with awesome pace assailed.
We well recall your mighty frame
All clad in white – a noble game
As you the willow there did wield
On many a distant playing field.

But then you left us – what commotion! –
For Wath-on-t'Dearne, where soon promotion
Transformed your somewhat urban scene
Up to the rank of Rural Dean,
A post you held with special grace
And beamed on all with smiling face.

Small wonder then that rightly you
Were chosen for some nobler pew,
And like my friend, good Canon Ball,
Now occupy t'Cathedral stall.
Grave and composed we see you there,
Tall, handsome, brave and debonair
Intoning Evensong (at 5)
With ancient canons (some alive)
Frowning on careless choir boys who

Are wont to chatter in the pew.
And as the choir some anthem sings
You'll dream perhaps of greater things?
A Sub-Dean or a Provost who
Inferior clergy will eschew.

Maybe your sights are set too low?
Perhaps as you more venerable grow
An archidiaconal post may come
Along your way? That would be fun!
Your knees, alas, (oh, cruel fate!)
Are in a rather parlous state
Which could inhibit you of course
From riding (gaitered) on a horse.
Maybe the Crown Appointments then
Will summon you to No. 10?
And Tony o'er a cup of tea
Will offer you a vacant see.
Her Majesty, we're glad to learn,
Has even heard of Wath-on-t'Dearne!
You'll look real 'cool'; oh, what a sighter,
At six feet four in t'cope and mitre.
As 'archiepisky' hands are laid
Upon your BALding head – be not dismayed!
There's many a cricketing cleric who
Has made it to the top, like you!
Clad in fine purple on the bench,
You'll catch the eye of many a wench.
But if you catch the Primate's eye
Then further honours we espy.
We've even heard (no idle talk)
You're hotly tipped to go to York.
And, should you follow Dr Hope,
You may be nominated Pope!

Meanwhile, dear Mart (I'm getting tired)
Canons we know can well be fired,
And from their lofty perch may fall,
And land up as a Canon Ball!

The Rev'd Martin Baldock

Martin Baldock was a fellow curate and cricketer from Nailsea, pro-
moted to be Rural Dean of Wath-on-Dearne. He was an awesome 6' 4"
tall fast bowler who represented the Diocese of Bath and Wells and
was a fellow member of the team in the period 1978-84.

Dear Martin, what is this we learn,
You're Rural Dean of Wath-on-Dearne?
Preferment comes now thick and fast,
The age of miracles ain't past!
But you (of all incumbents) most
Deserve this quite prestigious post.
The local press with wild acclaim
Hath blazoned forth your growing fame!
Clad in biretta, cassock, cope,
You'll look (we think) just like the Pope!
When churchmen (high) their antics play,
Causing you moments of dismay,
You, from your loft six foot four
Will bring them well to heel, we're sure!
And when you're feeling much incensed,
Let discipline be swift dispensed.
All clerics, erring from the norm,
We know you'll gently them reform.
For they true piety must learn
From Martin, Dean of Wath-on-Dearne!

To Jim Challis

Written from St Julian's Retreat House, Coolham, Sussex

This is a light-hearted poem to a very dear friend who cared for his elderly mother till she was 102. The end part is a serious reflection on a real ministry of costly caring.

Dear Jim – you rang, but all in vain,
And spoke instead to Mrs Payne.
The 'Nether regions' I'd forsaken
And had instead a journey taken
To this retreat where I come oft.
They've quartered me up in the loft
Or attic chamber where I lie
'Twixt heaven and earth, beneath the sky.
Here waited on by lovely girls
Who powder my once golden curls.
Enfolded in such loving care
I rest content within my lair,
While you, dear James, no respite have
From labours oft in Ryders Ave.
The ceaseless round, the common task,
Is what you scarcely thought to ask
When you retired ten years ago.
Did you e'er dream it would be so?

Now three score years and more have fled
And we have heard 'tis widely said,
There's no home help in Thanet who
In skill and wisdom rivals you!
Adept as cook and washing too,
There's really nothing you can't do!
Smart on the draw-sheet, none is quicker
When changing undersheet or knicker.

As medic and physician bold
Your prowess now is widely told.
And in 'commodious' situation
Remarkable your power of levitation.

So as housekeeper, domestic, maid,
You've soldiered on with little aid,
Save for an hour at morn and eve
When two good ladies you relieve.
And some week-ends which can be dreary
Your good kind friend, the lovely Mary,
Who a sweet ray of sunshine blessed
Affords you just a little rest.
Oh, did I hear a voice say, "Honey!
Do pop upstairs and dust the Monet".)
The daily round, the common task,
It seems an awful lot to ask.
At moments should you p'raps despair,
Remember His most loving care,
Who took a towel and water sweet
And washed twelve pairs of dirty feet.
Such acts of service he'd applaud
As rendered to our courteous Lord.
So as you daily seek his face,
Know he supplies all needed grace.

To A Damsel In Distress

This was placed on the car of a lady, unknown to us previously, whose car had broken down. My wife, Anne, and I helped her to start.

Dear Celia,

Your kindly note at last we found
Beneath our wipers, safe and sound,
And opened it with trembling hand
Lest it might be a reprimand
For parking on another's space,
Which could have led to our disgrace.
Instead we found your courteous note
Which you so kindly to us wrote.

We'd heard your car in some distress
And saw you in a sorry mess.
With choke and roar and grunt and splutter,
You might have landed in the gutter!
But hastening to your aid we ran,
A lady and a gentleman.
Both OAPs, yet not too frail
To follow closely on your trail.
We there applied our combined weight
And pushed your car with all our might.
With joy we heard the engine start
And watched you gladly then depart.
Such joy it was – (surely you guess?) –
To help a 'damsel in distress'!

And now your Polo is repaired
We're glad we just one minute spared.
Forgive this rather long rendition,
We trust your car's in **MINT** condition!

Sits Vac

This is a 'send up' of a fellow cricketer, John Reed, after his suggested appointment as Dean of St Albans.

Scanning "Church Times" my eye did glance
Upon a Vacant Deanery perchance.
Forgive me if I seem too nosey,
The Deanery is warm and cosy,
And (Moore's the pity) Peter goes.
If John should Reed, I don't suppose
He might be lured by sound of bells
From sojourning in Bath and Wells?

The team's bereft (I've said before)
We need a watchful No. 4.
And knowing well your skills at cricket
Suggest, St. Albans: return ticket!
With watchful eye upon the scene
We think you'd make a splendid Dean
And from your mediaeval stall
Would keep your eye upon the ball.

Now Timsbury's loss: Verulamium's gain!
Or have I writ these words in vain?
A Crown Appointment! Should you be keen,
We'll have a quiet word with the dear Queen.
And for success, I'll surely wager,
You'll have support from good John Major.
For he of all PMs we know
Just loves the game that you love so.
And should your overtures succeed,
You'll be The Very Rev John Reed!

Oh, My Foot!

Easter 1987

*This is a light-hearted poem written after a dear friend, James, sustained
a nasty accident to his foot.*

To James McP the vision came
To build for Sarah's dainty frame
At House of Cleaves, a country seat
Where, after hours, they both could meet
And gaze, when life might seem forlorn,
Like Ruth upon the alien corn,
And shedding pedagogic cares might rest
And look upon the woodland blessed,
And there the distant hills survey
And learn to pause at close of day.

This rustic seat our James must build,
So he with stone the barrow filled,
While Charlie lent a steadying hand,
Father and son, O happy band!
But, (reader, please prepare for shock),
Whilst they did heave that ancient rock
It slipped from 'neath their conjoined hand
And on poor James' foot did land!

A cry went up that rent the skies,
(For guessing what he said, no prize!)
For none save Charles shall ever know
What imprecations from Dad's lips did flow.
Wood pigeons startled from their roost
Fled in confusion, panic-loosed,
While pheasants whirred and oxen blared
As man and beast the mayhem shared.

Fair Sarah ran to where he lay,
A bleeding victim, cold and grey.
The woodlands wept, the skies were hushed
As he lay prostrate, groaning, crushed.
"Oh, James", quoth she, "Did I not say
That if with stones you boys must play
And seek to build my rustic seat,
Oh, do be careful of your feet!"

"Oh, prithee Sarah, say no more
Whilst I am lying on the floor,
But call the doctor, fairest sweet,
And get me off my rustic seat."
To Southmead Casualty they came
On Easter Eve, with halt and lame,
And there the bleeding foot, I state,
They nearly had to amputate.

But surgeons skilled did ply their art
And saved the disaffected part.
X-rays revealed (beneath the groans)
Some broken metatarsal bones.
With soothing hand and gentle touch
They bandaged him from toe to crutch.
And though no plaster was applied
They reckon that he nearly died.

Transported home by sorrowing wife,
Despairing of her James' life,
They lifted him by hands and feet
And laid him on his rustic seat.
And there beside the House of Cleaves
They covered him with autumn leaves.

Now what transpired on Easter Eve
None shall e'er know and few believe.
He came to church on Easter Day
With Sarah fair and children twae.
And some in congregation said,
"'Tis resurrection of the dead!"

The moral though for James is clear,
And all who cherish loved ones dear,
That when you build a rustic seat
Oh, <u>do</u> be careful of your feet!

Bathroom Siege

At No. 3, The Glebe

This is largely factual but with a humorous and fictional ending.

When tenancy had long since lapsed
And April skies were blue,
The landlord and his lady rode
To Wrington – parlez-vous?

MacPhersons (J and S) declared,
"School bills must soon be paid."
For mortgage rates were climbing high,
And so was a fair young maid!

To interview some tenants new
Appointments had been made.
So to No. 3 they drove to see
What plans could there be laid.

The cottage (No. 3 The Glebe)
Was empty all agreed.
So early they arrived that day –
The saga please now read:

When James did boldly ope' the door
Imagine his surprise
When he did spy a load of gear
Stacked up before his eyes.

Each passage and each corridor
With cases was piled high.
And "Gosh!" said he, and "Gosh!" said she,
"We can't imagine why!"

But just imagine how they felt
When laughter could be heard
From deep within the bathroom suite,
A man with a pretty young bird!

"Who's there?", cried James. The voices ceased,
And silence reigned within
Those bathroom walls where the shadow falls.
And now does my tale begin.

For James looked up, and of what he saw
We can only now just speak.
'Twas a maiden fair with a mop of hair
And a blush on her maiden cheek.

"Pray, who are you?" James boldly asked,
And she quite shocked replied,
"I'm the tenant, as you see, of No. 3",
And she blushed like a honeymoon bride.

"Oh, tell me another!" said James, abashed
At the sight of the pretty young maid
Half clad in a 'robe du bain' forsooth,
Leaving rather too much displayed.

"And who's the gentleman with you there,
Whose laughter could be heard?
He may be fickle, yet I guess likes a tickle
With a scarcely-fledged young bird!

"I'm the tenant bold, and in truth I was told
That this cottage was free to rent.
The Agent has my name and address
And quite honourable's my intent.

The gentleman's the valet at The Glebe.
Attending all mishaps,
He's in the bathroom in the plumber's role
Attending to the bathroom taps."

"Come, come!" said James, "You can't expect
A headmaster to be naïve.
I ask you forsooth to tell me the truth,
A pedagogue you can't deceive!"

Arbitration was sought, they settled out of court.
An agreement has now been made.
Though times are thin, yet the rent's coming in
And the mortgage is nearly paid!

The sequel to the story I fear is rather hoary,
It may even occasion some frowns.
The gent and the maid for their error have paid –
They've entered him now for 'The Downs'!

Birthday Verses

To Ken Ramsay, Lee Abbey, 1958.

These were written for The Rev'd Ken Ramsay's 40th birthday. He was ribbed for constructing a 'kissing gate' when still a bachelor.

Our Kenneth is now twenty-one
(He looks not a day more than forty!)
Though he smiles with the grace of a nun
We know that at heart he's still naughty.

Though his pate be half bald and he's greying
(The tonsure has hidden the worst),
We know that his heart goes a-maying
And of 'gallantes' we vote him the first.

For our Kenneth we know will not harden
His heart, for we have heard how in rags
He confessed on his knees to the Warden
He still loves Miss Polly-thene Bags!

But what would you like for your birthday?
Oh, pray do not tell us too late!
May we humbly suggest there's a dearth, say,
Of sites for a new kissing gate?

Bath and Wells Clergy Cricket Dinner 1988

This is a 'send up' of our Clergy cricket team who, in 1988, were dismissed for an ignominious 29. The following year we were narrowly 'pipped' in the final by two runs!

I tell the tale tonight of those
Whose promise faded like the rose.
With heads unbowed yet bloody, they
Were glorious on that awful day
When, humbled by proud London's might,
They'd sensed that victory was in sight.
'Two-nine all out' is not so fine,
But we'll come good in '89,
And proudly at Southgate will stand
With Church Times Cup in Michael's hand!

When Michael bats at No. 1
We know he'll graft for every run.
Neat, dapper, polished, watchful, he
Will nudge, deflect, defend and see
If there be movement, seam, or bounce,
Yet gladly on the loose ball pounce
With cover drive or neat leg-glance,
We'll slowly watch his score advance.
And there beneath the mid-day sun
We know he's counting every run.
And he, our donnish Ph.D,
May still be there long after tea!

Down at the other end, perchance,
We'll see young Ader's score advance.
With neat deflection, cracking drive
He'll at his 50 soon arrive.
This village lad from far-off Stoke-
Sub-Hamdon says, "it is no joke,
Year-in, year-out through summer days

To partner 'Maestro' Michael Hayes.
Yet now restored by surgeon's knife,
We look for resurrection life!"

And entering now at No. 3
A man of class we surely see.
Like David Gower (yet not so fair)
It's Richard, tall and debonair.
With watchful skill and easeful grace
Dispatching balls of furious pace,
Panache and elegance we see,
Proud member of the MCC!
What shall we say of David Jeans
Whose lately vanished from the scene?
The spinner's art he'll ply no more
For Bath and Wells, so we implore
Your Lordship, please, we humbly pray
That you and Bishop George soon may
Ordain young men and grace impart
To weave the spinner's magic art.

There's No. 4 whose cause I plead,
It is our batsman good John Reed.
Pipe-sucking scholar, Timsbury Saint,
He is a batsman of restraint.
Content to graft there all day long
And gently nudge the score along.
A man not given to taking risks,
Especially with his lumbar discs!

When Martin B comes thundering in
It is a very awesome thing.
With flailing arms and pounding feet
We watch the batsmen in retreat.
The slips fall back, the keeper quails,
For fear of flying stumps or bails.
With swinging yorker, aerial wide,
Big Bird's the terror of the side!
When spirits fail and hearts grow sick

We know that we can turn to Dick.
Bald and bespectacled with beard
He is a bowler greatly feared.
Shirt-tail a-flapping in the breeze
The timely wicket he will seize
With subtle use of swing and seam.
He is the member of our team
Who, when the chances are put down,
Will never rant or rave or frown,
But with a smile both kind and mellow
Will kindly mutter, "Hard luck, fellah!"

There's Colin, too, of fiery pace,
The lad from Worle, with boyish face.
When bowling off his longer run
He's lost beneath the Weston sun!
When wearied to his mark he'll stroll,
A cry goes up, "Good on yer, Col!"

And then there's John (Sebastian) Coe,
A man whom many of you know.
Though not so mobile on his pins
Will field each ball upon his shins!
While in the covers he doth lurk
The crunching drive he will not shirk.
For round his shins there's carpet rolled,
The finest Axminster we're told!

What shall I say of brother Paul,
Whose greyhound excellence we all
Applaud? Swift on the speeding ball he'll seize
With bounding elegance and ease.
He'll clutch it from the furthest picket
And hurl it (full toss) to the wicket
Where keeper Michael (5 foot nil)
Will neatly catch it, and then still
Whip off the bails and cry, "Howzat?"
The erring batsman knows that's that!
And what of him, the 'ancient bard',

The one whose ageing frame is scarred
With battle wounds on fields of play
Full fifty summers (so some say).
Yet like a greyhound in the slips
He'll snatch and strain, yet sometimes grips
The speeding ball, and with a shout
Of sheer amazement cry, "That's out!"
Shall he not run who writ this piece
From pole to pole till runs shall cease?

And some there be (I dread to say)
With no memorial this day.
They are the unknown warriors who
Will umpire, score, tea duties do,
Without a murmur or complaints.
These have the hall-marks of the saints,
And though not chosen as the XI
Will surely find reward in heaven!

But, please, before the autumn's over
Just take a tip from Alfred Gover.
His indoor school has 'winter lets',
We'll see you shortly in the nets!

Any Old Bones

This is a 'send up' of Fosamax which is often prescribed for osteoporosis.

For bones which crumble and decay
Medecine hath shone the light of day.
And weary men, midst toil and strife,
Are promised Resurrection Life.

That which the bone so sadly lacks
Can be restored by Fosamax.
A daily dose at half past seven
Can prove indeed a taste of heaven.
So rise from your bid, though pale and wan,
And take your medecine like a man!

Also Ran

St Leger

This is a 'send up', with names changed.

Ride a cock horse to Banbury Course,
But Tom cannot ride any faster.
We'll back him each way for a penny a day
In pursuit of the fair Mary Master.

Ride a cock horse to Banbury Course,
Tom cannot ride any faster.
There's many a tot without wrinkle or spot
But none for sheer beauty surpassed her!

Ride a cock horse to Banbury Course,
Tom cannot ride any faster.
He's romping away from the field on this day
In pursuit of the fair Mary Master.

Ride a cock horse to Banbury Course,
Tom cannot ride any faster.
There's a gap by the rails and past her he sails –
I think he is courting disaster!

Ride a cock horse to Banbury Course,
Tom cannot go any faster.
Though he's handsome and tall, I fear he may fall
For the nice looking filly, Miss Master.

Ride a cock horse to Banbury Course,
But Tom cannot ride any faster.
At Beecher's he fell, and I'm sorry to tell
A story that ends in disaster.

The moral is clear, as you wipe back a tear,
As life's lessons so harshly do teach us:
When you go for a ride leave the fillies aside,
You may well come a cropper at Beecher's!

125 Not Out

For the "Church Times" 125th anniversary
by a CT Cup cricketer 1977

The names included are former editors of the Church Times. Happily Mr
Palmer is still with us. A small part of the poem was published in the
Church Times.

D ear Editor, I write with fear
To say in this auspicious year
That your fine innings (still 'not out')
Is some achievement, without doubt.
One twenty-five is quite a score,
We hope that there'll be many more.
Perhaps before your day is done
You may record a 'double ton'?
(The Aussies bi-centenary
Is a reminder salutory.)
We hope that those on whom you call
With pen and ink (like bat and ball)
Are mindful of the days by-gone
And keep the score board ticking on.

We would recall on this fair page
Those who first graced the golden age,
Giants of old in sunnier climes
Who batted first for the "Church Times".
Men like the Palmers who inspire
Good Henry J and George Josiah.
Some saw the light of E H Day,
While others sadly had to play
Their finest innings (my words mark!)
Like Sidney, groping in the Dark.
Yet others lacking such Prestige
Were 'caught behind' in war-time siege.
When war was past and Heath had gone
The faithful Humphry Beevored on.

The fifties flowered with Rosamund
The fair Essex (oh, help, I've punned!)
With R L Roberts (what a charmer)
We pass on now to Bernard Palmer,
The one whose name like Father Time
Adjudicates this rambling rhyme,
The last and most illustrious Player
To fill the editorial chair.

And so the innings now has crept
Past 125, and you have kept
A kind and friendly watch we know
Upon the players as they go.
In this good year of grace divine,
Pray, will you be our Valentine?
And though we know you're not a pup
Kindly accept the Church Times Cup!

Toothless In Thanet

This is a light-hearted 'send up' of a dear friend who inadvertently left his plate down the bed after staying with us.

Dear James, I am writing now to say
That as you hurried on your way
One priceless gift you left behind,
(For out of sight is out of mind).

A denture with three teeth (no less)!
We fear you're in a sorry mess
And (pray forgive this poor rendition)
Somewhat, well, lacking in dentition.

Our dental knowledge is quite slim,
(But you'll forgive us, dearest Jim).
A molar and two canines, is it
You left in bed, after your visit?

Now, chewing ageing beef or pork
You'll find it rather hard to talk.
So, God of the Gaps, have mercy do
And help our aged friend to chew!

Of teeth bereft it must be tough,
Of gnashing gums you've had enough.
So we return the 'family plate',
Fearing you're in an awful state.

But now rejoice! And say a prayer
For those who follow in your lair.
But for my wife's discerning eye,
They might have had a painful lie
Within the guest room and have said,

"My bottom's blue, my cheeks are red,
For something bit me in the dark,
And here to prove it is the mark
Of an intruder in the night
Who gave me such a fearsome bite."

So we enclose, with a donation,
Something to aid your mastication.
Pray now accept the missing teeth
That could have caused untimely death.

Life's never easy, sad to state,
You cannot 'have it on a plate'.
And as with years you grow yet wiser,
Take care of molar and incisor!

Ode To The Rural Dean

*This is a light-hearted riposte to a Vicar who forbade the erection of a
small toilet in his Vicarage garden.*

The Rural Dean (your blushes spared)
Has now his solemn will declared:
"My garden fair shall not be used
Or by the public be abused
For 'privy purposes' forsooth.
No closet, loo, or humble booth
Shall you erect, nor therein build.
Nor though your hands be amply skilled
Will I permit this plot to be
A kind of public WC.
As I have fully now explained
Your earthly needs must be restrained".
It's published in the magazine,
Such thoughts are really quite obscene.
The Rector's freehold doth preclude
Such usage, common, coarse and crude.
As Herrick wrote long years ago,
(His verses you must surely know),
"A garden is a lovesome thing",
And while its praises we shall sing
Bill hath decreed (as sure you wot)
"Thou shalt not tiddle on my plot,
Nor scent the rosebush as you pass
Or tinkle (quietly) on the grass.
Nor shall you dig the heaving sod,
It is reserved for me (and God)."
The apple trees that lean down low
For ever undisturbed shall grow,

And so this hamlet's "Linden Lea"
Is <u>not</u> the place for you to pee.
And should you hear fair nature's call
We kindly ask you not to fall
Into the error some have made,
The roses (note) have all been sprayed!

And so the congregation's plea
To have exclusive rights to pee
Has been refused; a summons will
Be served on all who tiddle still.
Bill Smithers (Rev) M.A., R.D.,
Has issued forth his last decree.
Who dare oppose this bold fiat?
It's printed now – nihil obstat!

Ode To Mr White

This was written for my niece, Jane, who had a much-loved toy polar bear, Mr White.

Oh! Mr White,
I think you're quite
Enchanting!
Your funny paws
I just adores,
They set me panting!

Your soft brown eyes
So kind and wise
Just get me twitching.
And when you wink
I kinda think
You're – well – bewitching!

Oh! Mr White,
You know I'm quite
Besotted.
For when you smile
All bearophile,
My downfall's surely plotted!

Your shining teeth
Are like a wreath
Of pearls from ocean distant.
Ope wide your throat,
I'll stand and dote
This very instant.

Your furry ears
Move me to tears,
I thee adore,
Like Acker Bilky!

Oh! Mr White,
You know I'm quite
Besotted.
And when you smile
I'd run a mile,
My heart strings knotted!

Ice caps would melt
If I just knelt
Before your feet adoring.
For love on ice
There is no price,
Pray, hear my heart's outpouring.

My heart was cold,
But I've been told
Your love warms icebergs yearly.
With love unfrozen
Pray be my chosen,
You know I love you dearly!

Oh! Mr White,
You know I'm quite
Besotted!
Of love (like cream)
I lie and dream,
My arteries with love are clotted!

And then (words fail)
I love your tail,
It's so divinely charming.
My heart grows bold,
Is our tale told?
I find it quite alarming!

Oh! Mr White,
My troth I'll plight,
Whate'er betide thee.
'Neath polar moon
I'll stay and swoon,
Love-sick beside thee!

Such love on ice
Can know no price,
My ardent love o'erflowing.
Through ebb and flow
You'll surely know
Which way the wind is blowing.

Your furry frame,
I say (sans shame)
Sets my heart beating.
And should you growl
I'd sit and howl,
My precious sweeting!

When skies were grey
I used to stay
At home with my dear mother.
Now you're the bear
For whom I care
Above all other.

My furry paws
I'll place in yours
And we'll go dancing
Upon the ice,
Silent as mice,
We'll glide romancing!

We'll dance all night
And I will plight
My heart to you, my chosen.
'Neath arctic moon
We'll stay and swoon
Amidst the pack ice frozen!

Oh! Mr White,
Love at first sight
Has sent me reeling!
Can this be true?
My love for you
Is such a strange romantic feeling.

So, Mr White,
I think it's right
To say, "I love you dearly."
Shall we get wed
And make our bed
Within some bear den duly?

Dear Mr White,
You've set alight
A love flame none can stifle.
No killer whale
Can love assail
Nor dreaded hunter's rifle!

So, Mr White,
My troth I plight
With bear hugs so romantic.
As groom and bride
Let's catch the tide
And sail across the Atlantic!

Ode To Bill Frindall

On his engagement to Miss Deborah Brown

This is a light-hearted poem dedicated to Bill Frindall, the veteran cricket commentator known as 'The Beard'.

O William, alias The Beard,
Can we believe what we have heard?
We thought you proudly chauvinistic
Yet you've provided one statistic
Wisden at least can n'eer dispute:
You clearly found Miss Brown a beaut,
And coached long years by Alfred Gover
At last have 'bowled a maiden over'!
From Canterbury's dark pavilion
You picked a girl, one in a million.

So Cupid, using all his wiles,
The bearded wonder now beguiles,
For she who's dubbed the lovely 'Handers'
To gastronomic taste now panders.
While others on plain grub have choked
She plies you well with salmon (smoked).
The commentator's box it seems
Has now fulfilled your wildest dreams.
While with statistics you still wrestle
You've clearly picked a 'Test Match Special'!

If panic now your soul assails,
Consider 'Canterbury Tales':
No longer now a Freeman, you
All other maidens must eschew
And ere we come to Feb two nine
Remember please a Valentine.
Consider well your chosen lot

Before you tie the fatal Knott.
The score book you must enter fully,
(Dost not you think my line unWoolley?)
And if the faintest doubt still lingers
Then have a word of prayer with 'Wingers'.

But be assured from all who play
Feb twenty-nine's 'Match of the Day'!

Ode To An Inventive Genius

Dedicated to the Rt Rev'd George Carey

This was dedicated to The Rt Rev George Carey, then recently consecrated as Bishop of Bath and Wells. He inadvertently forgot his clerical collar on the way up to Westminster Abbey.

When on the journey up to town
Our Bishop George was seen to frown
It was because one thing he lacked:
No collar (clerical) he'd packed.

What should he do with train in motion?
To sound the alarm would cause commotion,
To pull communication cord
Was something he could ill afford.

He left his seat, with door ajar,
And sidled to the Buffet Car.
And plucking all his courage up
He seized a plastic BR cup.

Then stealing down the corridor
Discreetly closed the toilet door.
'Engaged' it said. Engaged in what?
And here began the artful plot.

While engine roared and carriage shook
His Lordship (holding fast his crook)
Did there contrive with skill and passion
A collar (clerical) to fashion.

With scissors sharp he then cut up
The aforesaid plastic BR cup.
And when the train through Reading passed
All Wippell's skills he'd far surpassed!

As engine roared and carriage rocked
The dread deed's done (in privy locked).
Tip-toeing back on silent feet
He quietly then resumed his seat.

No passing guard or e'en dumb waiter
Did spot the change, 'twas only later
Did they discern, when clearing up,
A mutilated plastic cup.

The Bishop now, his journey done,
Alighted (late) at Paddington.
And clad with collar hailed a cabby
To drive him hot-foot to the Abbey.

And there 'midst brethren all parsonical
Adorned himself in 'Full Canonical'.
The Verger smiled, the Primate beamed,
But which of fellow Bishops dreamed

That he was clad, as in 'full mail',
By courtesy of British Rail!
The Primate bet his bottom dollar
He'd never seen a finer collar!

Did those who then were Bishops made
Ever suspect when hands were laid
Upon their heads, all bowed and pale,
The grace was given through British Rail?

And so from Durham and Trinity too
We all give thanks for our Bishop who
In time of crisis kept his cool,
And even the Primate managed to fool!

The moral is clear and easy to follow:
If you've left behind your clerical collar
Then pray to the Lord and just look up
And lay your hands on a plastic cup!

He ne'er lost his nerve, nor did courage fail,
He signs himself now,

+ George, British Rail.

Ode For St Valentine's Day

Dedicated to the Provost of Barchester

This was published as a response to a senior cleric's dismissal of undue familiarity during the exchanging of The Peace.

Some congregations (it is feared)
Have had their reputations smeared,
Because 'The Peace' (I blush at this)
Has now become the place to kiss!
And men and maidens seeking grace
Are even daring to embrace.
No longer now they stiffly stand
And shake their neighbour's frozen hand.
Choir girls who once would coyly smile
Are seen advancing down the aisle
To plant a sweet and loving peck
Upon the dear Church Warden's neck.
And those who once would hardly speak
Are seen embracing cheek to cheek,
And hearts beat faster in the pew
Now this is what they've learned to do.

The Provost says, "Enough's enough!"
And though you find his strictures tough
We kindly ask you to refrain
From kissing in 'The Peace' again.
We think that you will now agree
It's really not quite C of E.

And so the fun and games must cease
Or you'll be done for breach of peace.
But, Provost dear, though we shall miss
That moment of the holy kiss,
I ask of you one treasured sign:

Pray will you be my Valentine?

Lo! He Comes With Clouds Descending

Dedicated to David Powell MBE, Parachutist Extraordinary
1997

This was written for my beloved cousin, David Powell, now in his 90th year, on achieving a remarkable free-fall parachute jump. He plans to repeat this shortly.

A veteran, David Powell by name,
Has set our craven hearts aflame
With deeds of courage that would shame
Most men of lesser years.

From 14,000 feet this clown
Hath safely parachuted down.
His epic deed, talk of the town,
Hath moved grown men to tears.

Strapped to his brave instructor Max,
He travelled faster than a fax.
In 'daring-do' he nothing lacks
This lad of eighty years.

Grandad and man of noble birth,
A man of undiminished girth,
He fairly whistled down to earth,
Arousing all our fears.

Circling above the airfield he
Above the clouds we scarce could see.
But then he spread his canopy,
And raised the cry, "Three cheers!"

Martha gazed up to see her Pa
Descending from the skies afar,
And shouted out, "Oh, well done, Da!"
And wiped away her tears.

Did William Abbott (from his grave)
Look up and give a passing wave,
With some such words, "Good on yer, Dave,
Not bad for eighty years!"

The Royal Marines and lads from Dido
(Recalling Operation Fido)
Salute you for your freefall rido,
Young lad of eighty years.

Veteran of Copenhagen, he
Without a doubt we all agree
Deserves at least an OBE
(Washed down with Tubourgs beers).

So get out the drinks and serve the rum.
Splice the mainbrace, don't be glum,
He might have landed on his bum!
Young lad of eighty years.

Five thousand quid! That isn't bad
For sponsoring such a bearded lad.
And we all know the Dean is glad
To pay off some arrears.

The Trustees of the Appeal agree
You should be made an OBE,
An' it shall please her Majesty,
Young lad of eighty years.

The moral of this tale is clear:
To all who pre-senescence fear
Look up, old boy, reach for the skies,
You're heading for a glorious prize!

Hot Flush

I wake in the night with a terrible fright,
My blood coursing round in a rush.
I can feel my temp' rising, it's hardly surprising,
I think that I'm having a flush.

I wake hot and clammy, cry out "Oh, Mammy!"
I feel like a great burning bush.
Is it vasodilation or extreme agitation?
Yes, I fear that I'm having a flush.

My husband has said, "You must get out of bed",
But to do so would cause me to blush.
As I toss and I turn I can feel myself burn,
I fear that I'm having a flush.

I groan and I shout, he says "Darling, hop out!"
And I fear he will 'give me the push'.
As I sweat and I stutter I can hear him now mutter
"It's clear that you're having a flush".

I can't sleep a lot, I'm all sticky and hot,
Perspiration breaks out in a rush.
"My darling", he cries, "For guessing no prize,
I presume that you're having a flush".

I'm in a great state and I'm sad to relate
I cuss and I swear and say "Tush".
And the truth will soon dawn at the break of the morn,
I think I've been having a flush.

It's now beyond joking, my nightie is soaking,
This pasture is really too lush.
As I lie there and sweat all the bedclothes are wet,
I know that I'm having a flush.

Yes, the going is tricky, I'm all hot and sticky,
More blood through my system doth rush.
Oh, life is forlorn, will I cool off by dawn
And wake to the voice of the thrush?

If this is 'the change' then I'd rather exchange
My lot with some lavatory brush.
You may think me a fool but at least I'd be cool,
As it is, life is just one long flush!

Limericks

These were written 'sending up' various friends of mine over many years.

A romantic young salesman from Perth
Had a huge and immeasureable girth.
But I fear he was jilted –
His lass spied him kilted
And exclaimed, "You're an object of mirth!"

A graceful young dancer from Calais
Fell in love with a beau in the ballet.
When cruising to Dover
He bowled her right over,
A pas de deux? No, they're just pally!

An amorous young lady from Ely
Fell in love with a gent they call Healey.
But with love unrequited
Their troth was not plighted,
Alas! He was not 'touchy-feely'!

At a Festival staged down at Cannes
Two film stars in love called their banns.
Singing excerpts from "Tosca"
They gained but one Oscar,
And now they are dubbed 'also rans'

There was an old boy from Darjeeling
Who said, "Excess tea sends me reeling.
I fall on the deck

Crying, "Oh, what the heck!"
And lie there bereft of all feeling!"

There was a young fellah from Dunstable
Who was had up for assaulting a constable.
At the Magistrate's Court
The psychiatrist's report
Declared he was 'totally unstable'!

A flirtatious young curate from Dover
Behaved like a real Casanova.
But his wife blew the whistle,
Now he's sworn on the Missal
He'll only go rompies with Rover!

A millionaire blonde lass from Beccles
Was smothered all over with freckles.
But with too much hot sun
I fear she's undone,
With sunblock she's spent all her shekels!

A footballer called Rudi Gullet
Once swallowed a rather large mullet.
He declared, "Oh, my soul!
I have scored an own goal,
I suppose I must now bite the bullet!

Middle-Aged Spread
(AEP)

I have noticed of late, my dear Aggy,
Your waistline has gone a bit saggy.
Though it's patent enough
You're a fine piece of stuff,
I prefer you upholstered, not baggy!

Lovelorn

I'm in love with the Duchess of York,
She's rather a nice piece of pork.
Though warned by the clergy,
I call her 'dear Fergie',
And people are starting to talk!

Confession

I have fallen for Miss Purdon Coote,
I think she is rather a 'beaut'.
Though thousands ignore her
I simply adore her
And reckon she's cuter than cute.

To Lady Di

I've just seen the Princess of Wales,
She 'fair took the wind oot ma sails'.
'Midst royal alarms,
I've succumbed to her charms,
And now I am ready to Di!

I've just seen the fair Lady Di,
She gave me (I think) the glad eye.
I telephoned Charles
But he angrily snarls
"Oh, rubbish! It's only a fly!"

Terms of Endearment

My wife is a rare precious metal,
Yet one thing we really can't settle.
When I lay in her bosom
She calls me 'my blossom',
But I'd rather be just her 'sweet petal'.

To Miss Burbridge

When I first met my Staff Nurse Burbridge,
I noticed her beak had a ridge.
When I gave her a peck
She cried out, "Oo 'eck!
I'm a dove, my sweet love, not a pidge!"

To Miss Organ (Physio)

When I first set my eyes on fair Kate,
My quadriceps was in a state.
But thanks to her skill
I am walking, and still
They've promised they'll not amputate.

Eyes Right! (St Julian's)

I have led my dear wife quite a dance,
No wonder she's looking askance.
Instead of the mallard
I've spotted Miss Callard,
And, my! She is worth a sly glance!

Staff Nurse Burbridge Protests

When I first set my eyes on Miss B
She took little notice of me.
But dragged to the sluices
She cried, "No excuses!
I think you're uncommonly free!"

Ill Bread?

I must have been born in the gutter
For I simply love peanutty butter.
But I really can't chew it,
So now must eschew it,
It gives me a t-terrible stutter.

Ode to Margaret

A sister from Southmead called Maggs,
Said, "Hi folks! I'm packing my bags.
I'm off on my scooter,
So find a new tutor,
And to ……. with those bloomin' old hags!"

Jim Challis

I'm sorry my writing's all shakers,
It's because I was schooled by the Quakers.
Though I shiver and shake
Please make no mistake
It is cordially signed, 'your old Akers'.

Birthday Ode
Margaret Leonard, 90 on 30 April 1989

We're glad that you've opened your hampers
For your health's sake please drink up the 'champers'.
At three score and twenty
You may drink it in plenty,
But don't cause a riot on the campus!

A tycoon from upper-crust Bushey
Was ruthless, ambitious and pushy.

When his employer struck
He declared, "I'm dumb struck"
They replied, "You've had it too cushy!"

A Scotsman just outside of Troon
Was greatly upset by the moon.
And a lunar eclipse?
Well, it gave him the 'gyps',
I fear he's collapsed in a swoon.

A Welshman who swam o'er the Usk
Succumbed to a bad dose of 'husk'.
He coughed and he spluttered,
But the doctor just muttered,
"I fear he'll expire before dusk!"

A native of far Belarus
Was attacked by a vicious mongoose.
As he cried out for help
He expired with a yelp:
"Oh, crikey! My head's in a noose!"

A drunkard whose name was Tom Kember
Fell ill on the 9th of September.
A confirmed alcoholic
He was labelled melancholic
And expired on the last day of December!

A saucy Professor from Dover
On the quiet was a real Casanova.
The girls said his charms
Caused them all wild alarms,
They'd rather have 'rompies' with Rover!

An eccentric zoologist from Rhodes
Had a terrible phobia of toads.
He would shriek and would stutter
And crouch in the gutter
Which offended the best Highway Codes.

A pigeon from distant Peru
Caused one hell of a hullabaloo.
When swallowing a mullet
It ruptured its gullet
And succumbed to an 'abortive coo'!

Ode To Charlie

(With apologies to Stanley Holloway)

Written and recited by the Rev. David Payne, Rector of Wraxall, at Saint Bartholomew's Harvest Supper at Failand on Saturday 24 September 1988. Charles and Arlene Crawshaw were guests and were presented with an inscribed goblet to mark Charles' 50th anniversary of his ordination.

There's a dearly loved church down yon hillside,
Which is famous for fresh air and fun,
Where the Reverend Charles Crawshaw as locum
Has often our church duty done.
He didn't think much to the singing,
The choir boys were lacking or dumb,
And the offertory procession's a nonsense,
"I'll sort thee out soon ..... 'ee by gum!"
They'd hardly processed down the nave like,
When a voice from on high shouted, "Stop!
You can't keep that organ a-thundering,
Young Michael, you'd best pack it up.
For I can't hear m'self speaking
While you lot are singing along.
I like you to pause in the midst, folks,
And <u>then</u> you continue your song."

Now when it do come to the sermon
Our Charles is not like Rector Payne,
He won' wrap it up mealy-mouthed like,
He prefers to speak it out plain.
"That space up aloft in the roof there
Is really – well, rather a joke.
Why don't you put in a false ceiling
And build sheltered housing for old folk?

Or maybe you'd pull out the pews, too,
And build a dance floor for the lads,
You're far too conservative and cautious,
You want to get rid of your fads!
This church is most beautiful Gothic
And, though it were lovingly made,
You can worship as well up the chancel
While the nave is a shopping arcade!"

Such bold, brave, outrageous suggestions
Our Charlie's been known to promote,
And though we protest, "He's a scandal",
In secret, on him we all dote.
We think he's a breath of fresh air, lads,
And whenever he comes we all vote
That this rugged, warm-hearted Lancastrian
Is really a guy of some note.
Though he shocks and surprises us often,
He drops all his bombs wi' a smile,
And we love you, dear Charles, you old rascal,
(We trust you'll hang on for a while!)

Tonight we have come to say 'thank you'
To God for your fifty long years.
For we know that the Lord has been faithful
And kept you through laughter and tears.
Yes, we've come to say, 'Thank you', dear Charlie,
For fifty years serving the Lord.
And we pray that supported by Arlene
You'll be blessed as you walk in his Word.

Ode To The Man In The Moon

In deepest sympathy, and by kind permission of Jodrell Bank, Mt Palomar Observatory, and the Astronomer Royal, marking the first moon landing in 1958.

Sing, Hi Davy Crockett,
Kruschev launched a rocket,
He launched it to land on the Moon.
Now observers record
That as moonwards it soared,
Certain nebulae fell in a swoon.
Orion held his belt
As he saw the smile melt
From the face of the Man in the Moon.

The Milky Way clotted
As the veins became knotted
On the brow de l'Homme de la Lune.
And the Pleiades wept
As the satellite swept
T'word the ill-fated Man in the Moon.
While Mars in convulsion
Cried, "Newton's repulsion
Is over and done with, you goon."
One and all did they cringe
As the lunatic fringe
Was scorched from la tete de la Lune.

But the Old Man yelled, "Niet!
Satellites ain't my diet,
Pop along to the Sun, you baboon."
And the Little Bear laughed
For the rocket shot aft

Of the face of the Man in the Moon.
And Venus observed
How the rocket had swerved
As it passed au dessus de la Lune.
Said Old Father Saturn,
"So this is the pattern
Of Kruschev's attempt to buffoon.
It's a poor sort of taxi
To invade my galaxy.
Ain't shooting stars cheaper at noon?"

Kruschev's missed the mark, it
Appears, and the target
Must wait till a clear night in June.
So hush, Davy Crockett,
You simply can't rock it
With a square like the Man in the Moon.
Now Lovell in deck-chair
Re-writes his sixth lecture
As "Voyage au clair de la Lune".

To The Lady Isobelle

Another tribute appears on p. 100

Alas! This verse is penned too late
For Valentines to ponder,
For Feb 14 is off the screen,
Yet true love ne'er was fonder.

The winter's chill has done me ill
(My hands were numb and frozen).
I've missed the post! Yet drink a toast
To you in winter hosen!

Swans down the Thames no longer glide
(I guess the water's frozen).
Here's my advice: keep off the ice!
Your tiny feet are frozen.

The ice has formed, it heaves and groans,
Aside the shores of Amsel.
I know such pain down Felix Lane,
I yearn for you, fair damsel.

So long since last we met,
I really can't remember.
I'm willing though to place a bet
'Twas August or September.

I came once more to your fair shore
(I think it was November)
But (here I groan) the bird had flown!
Where to I can't remember.

In some boat-yard (life can be hard)
I guess your timbers shiver.
Did you but know my heart's aglow,
My pen is all a-quiver!

These winter months are long and dull,
The skies are grey and leaden.
For nuppence I would scrape your hull,
For ship-wreck I am headin'!

In some dry dock beyond the lock
Your shining planks are gleaming,
Your paintwork smart. I know the art
Of Cupid who's been scheming.

Your varnished frame (I say sans shame)
Has set my heart a-beating.
Come out of dock! Prepare for shock!
Turn off my central heating!

Spring-time has come! And you're not dumb,
Fair Lady Isobelle, sweet damsel.
Shake off dull sloth! There's room for both
Of us beside the Amsel.

Midst ebb and flow our love must grow
When Cupid is a-calling.
Forgive this verse (I could do worse)
My scansion is appalling!

But life's been hard. Pity the bard
Who pens these verses tender.
There's much in store. You're in for more!
Please don't return to sender.

These verses (late) I'm sad to state
Have caused me much confusion.
Is this too hard: I've lost the card!
Goodbye, my lost illusion!

All I can say: I've missed the day,
A sign of ploys by scheming Cupid.
Will you be mine, sweet Valentine,
Yours hopelessly, incredibly, quite stupid!

Very Bad Ballads

Lee Abbey, N. Devon, 1958

These were composed in 1958/9 'sending up' fellow members of the Lee Abbey Community, Lynton, North Devon. They will clearly mean little except to former members of the Community.

There was a young lady called Palmer,
Who though C.S.M. was a charmer.
She organised files,
Wedding matches, big smiles,
And for tinies she acted as Mama.

There was a musician called Ward,
Who said, "I am sure that the Lord
Would rather I preach
Than school-kiddies teach.
Meanwhile I shall tend the greensward."

There was a young lady called Liz,
Who existed on faith, hope and fizz.
As she wasted away
They said, "Measurements, pray?"
But she told them, "Just mind your own biz."

There once was a lady called Win,
Who said, "I do think 'tis gross sin
To consume a cream tea
As a sabbath day spree.
Should you do so, please tell next-of-kin."

There was a young lady called Biddy,
Whose basket work drove her quite giddy.
Who said, "Peter V knows"
And the angel the whole lot he diddy.

There was a rare plant called Madgwickia
Who loved frolics and fun and high kickia.
She was fully herself
At eleven or twelf,
But for us who're repressed 'tis much trickier.

There was a young feller called Wilf,
Who said, "I rejoice that the filf
That is laid by my fowls
Will occasion no scowls,
For 'tis keeping the soil in fine tilf."